CW01646491

KAPLAN PUBLISHING

EXTRA ONLINE RESOURCES INCLUDED

*NOW THIS EXAM KIT COMES WITH*

# *FREE ONLINE ACCESS*

*TO EXTRA RESOURCES AIMED AT HELPING YOU PASS YOUR EXAMS*

**IN ADDITION TO THE OFFICIAL QUESTIONS AND ANSWERS IN THIS BOOK, GO ONLINE AND EN-gage WITH:**

- Fixed Tests
- Interim Assessments
- Exam paper Guides
- Latest Official ACCA exam questions
- Answers updated to include legislation relevant to next exam
- Frequent and varied new additions to these resources - watch this space!

**And you can access all of these extra resources anytime, anywhere using your EN-gage account.**

## How to access your online resources

| | |
|---|---|
| If you are a Kaplan Financial tuition, full-time or distance learning student | You will already have an EN-gage account and these extra resources will be available to you online. You do not need to register again, as this process was completed when you enrolled. If having problems accessing online materials, please ask your course administrator. |
| If you purchased through Kaplan Flexible Learning or via the Kaplan Publishing website | You will automatically receive an e-mail invitation to EN-gage online. Please register your details using this e-mail to gain access to your content. If you do not receive the e-mail or book content, please contact Kaplan Flexible Learning. |
| If you are already a registered EN-gage user | Go to www.EN-gage.co.uk and log in. Select the 'add a book' feature and enter the ISBN number of this book and the unique pass key at the bottom of this card. Then click 'finished' or 'add another book'. You may add as many books as you have purchased from this screen. |
| If you are a new EN-gage user | Register at www.EN-gage.co.uk and click on the link contained in the e-mail we sent you to activate your account. Then select the 'add a book' feature, enter the ISBN number of this book and the unique pass key at the bottom of this card. Then click 'finished' or 'add another book'. |
| **Your Code and Information** | **This code can only be used once** for the registration of one book online. This registration will expire when the final sittings for the examinations covered by this book have taken place. Please allow one hour from the time you submitted your book details for us to process your request. |

ewEx-BHbl-XqXq-kzZq

For technical support, please visit www.EN-gage.co.uk

Professional Examinations

# Paper F2

# Management Accounting (MA)

# EXAM KIT

ACCA OFFICIAL PUBLISHER

KAPLAN PUBLISHING

**British Library Cataloguing-in-Publication Data**

A catalogue record for this book is available from the British Library.

Published by:

Kaplan Publishing UK

Unit 2 The Business Centre

Molly Millar's Lane

Wokingham

Berkshire

RG41 2QZ

ISBN: 978-1-84710-765-7



Printed in the UK by CPI William Clowes Beccles NR34 7TL.



***Acknowledgements***

The past ACCA examination questions are the copyright of the Association of Chartered Certified Accountants. The original answers to the questions from June 1994 onwards were produced by the examiners themselves and have been adapted by Kaplan Publishing.

We are grateful to the Chartered Institute of Management Accountants and the Institute of Chartered Accountants in England and Wales for permission to reproduce past examination questions. The answers have been prepared by Kaplan Publishing.

# CONTENTS



## Section



NEW **New features in this edition**

In addition to providing a wide ranging bank of practice questions, we have also included in this edition:

- Paper specific information and advice on exam technique.
- Our recommended approach to make your revision for this particular subject as effective as possible.

  This includes step by step guidance on how best to use our Kaplan material (Complete text, pocket notes and exam kit) at this stage in your studies.

You will find a wealth of other resources to help you with your studies on the following sites:

www.EN-gage.co.uk and www.**acca**global.com/students/

# INDEX TO QUESTIONS AND ANSWERS

## PRACTICE QUESTIONS

# EXAM TECHNIQUE

- **Do not skip any of the material** in the syllabus.
- **Read each question** *very* carefully.
- **Double-check your answer** before committing yourself to it.
- Answer **every** question – if you do not know an answer, you don't lose anything by guessing. Think carefully before you **guess**. The examiner has indicated that many candidates are still leaving blank answers in the real exam.
- If you are answering a multiple-choice question, **eliminate first those answers that you know are wrong**. Then choose the most appropriate answer from those that are left.
- Remember that **only one answer to a multiple-choice question can be right**. After you have eliminated the ones that you know to be wrong, if you are still unsure, guess. Only guess after you have double-checked that you have only eliminated answers that are *definitely* wrong.
- **Don't panic** if you realise you've answered a question incorrectly. Getting one question wrong will not mean the difference between passing and failing

## Computer-based exams – tips

- Do not attempt a CBE until you have **completed all study material** relating to it.
- On the ACCA website there is a CBE demonstration. It is **ESSENTIAL** that you attempt this before your real CBE. You will become familiar with how to move around the CBE screens and the way that questions are formatted, increasing your confidence and speed in the actual exam.
- Be sure you understand how to use the **software** before you start the exam. If in doubt, ask the assessment centre staff to explain it to you.
- Questions are **displayed on the screen** and answers are entered using keyboard and mouse. At the end of the exam, you are given a certificate showing the result you have achieved.
- In addition to the traditional multiple-choice question type, CBEs might also contain **other types of questions**, such as number entry questions, formula entry questions, and stem questions with multiple parts. There are also questions that carry several marks.
- You need to be sure you **know how to answer questions** of this type before you sit the exam, through practice.

# PAPER SPECIFIC INFORMATION

## THE EXAM

## FORMAT OF THE PAPER-BASED AND COMPUTER BASED EXAM

| | *Number of marks* |
|---|---|
| 40 compulsory multiple choice questions (2 marks each) | 80 |
| 10 compulsory short questions (1 mark each) | 10 |
| | 90 |

Total time allowed: 2 hours

Two mark questions will usually require you to make calculations in order to ascertain the correct answer and will comprise of the following answer types:

(i) Multiple choice with four options (A, B, C or D)
(ii) Require you to enter a numerical answer (CBE only)
(iii) Ask you to select two correct answers from a choice of four

The one mark questions will predominately be theory questions and will comprise the following:

(i) Multiple choice with either two or three options
(ii) True or false options
(iii) Yes or no options

## AIM

To develop knowledge and understanding of how to prepare and process basic cost and quantitative information to support management in planning and decision-making in a variety of business contexts.

## OBJECTIVES

On successful completion of this paper, candidates should be able to:

- explain the nature and purpose of cost and management accounting
- describe costs by classification, behaviour and purpose
- apply essential business mathematics and use computer spreadsheets
- explain and apply cost accounting techniques
- prepare and coordinate budgets and standard costing for planning, feedback and control
- use management accounting techniques to make and support decision-making.

- Two mark questions will usually comprise the following answer types:
  (i) Multiple choice with four options (A, B, C or D)

(ii) Require you to enter a numerical answer (CBE only)

(iii) Ask you to select two correct answers from a choice of four

- The one mark questions will predominately be theory questions and will comprise the following:

  (i) Multiple choice with either two or three options

  (ii) True or false options

  (iii) Yes or no options

- ACCA official statistics have shown that most students do not find the exam time pressured and that the 1 mark questions do not seem to be any easier than the 2 mark questions

**PASS MARK**

The pass mark for all ACCA Qualification examination papers is 50%.

## DETAILED SYLLABUS

The detailed syllabus and study guide written by the ACCA can be found at:

www.accaglobal.com/students/

# KAPLAN'S RECOMMENDED REVISION APPROACH

## QUESTION PRACTICE IS THE KEY TO SUCCESS

Success in professional examinations relies upon you acquiring a firm grasp of the required knowledge at the tuition phase. In order to be able to do the questions, knowledge is essential.

However, the difference between success and failure often hinges on your exam technique on the day and making the most of the revision phase of your studies.

The **Kaplan complete text** is the starting point, designed to provide the underpinning knowledge to tackle all questions. However, in the revision phase, pouring over text books is not the answer.

**Kaplan Online fixed tests** help you consolidate your knowledge and understanding and are a useful tool to check whether you can remember key topic areas.

**Kaplan pocket notes** are designed to help you quickly revise a topic area, however you then need to practice questions. There is a need to progress to full exam standard questions as soon as possible, and to tie your exam technique and technical knowledge together.

**The importance of question practice cannot be over-emphasised.**

The recommended approach below is designed by expert tutors in the field, in conjunction with their knowledge of the examiner.

The approach taken for the fundamental papers is to revise by topic area.

**You need to practice as many questions as possible in the time you have left.**

## OUR AIM

Our aim is to get you to the stage where you can attempt exam standard questions confidently, to time, in a closed book environment, with no supplementary help (i.e. to simulate the real examination experience).

Practising your exam technique on real past examination questions, in timed conditions, is also vitally important for you to assess your progress and identify areas of weakness that may need more attention in the final run up to the examination.

The approach below shows you which questions you should use to build up to coping with exam standard question practice, and references to the sources of information available should you need to revisit a topic area in more detail.

Remember that in the real examination, all you have to do is:

- attempt all questions required by the exam
- only spend the allotted time on each question, and
- get them at least 50% right!

Try and practice this approach on every question you attempt from now to the real exam.

# THE KAPLAN PAPER F2 REVISION PLAN

## Stage 1: Assess areas of strengths and weaknesses

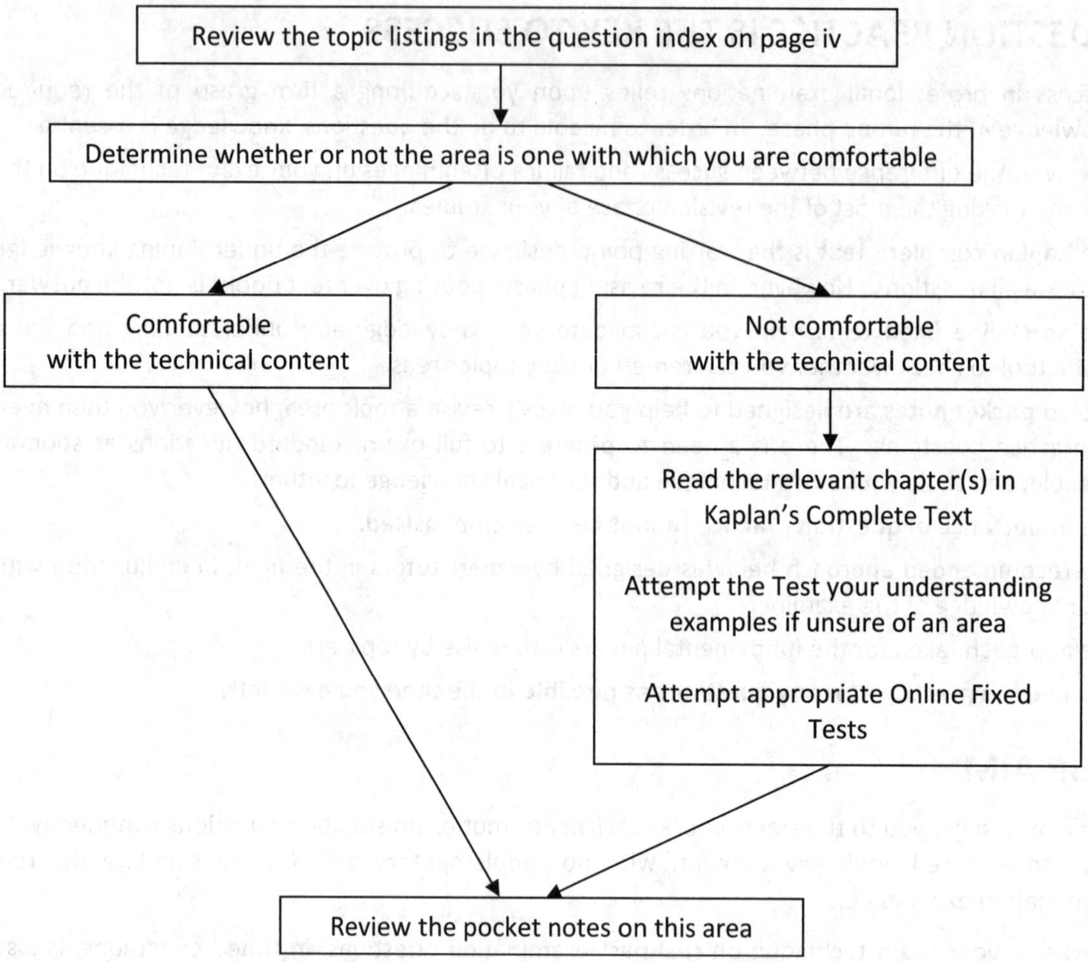


## Stage 2: Practice questions

Ensure that you revise all syllabus areas as questions could be asked on anything.

Try to avoid referring to text books and notes and the model answer until you have completed your attempt.

Try to answer the question in the allotted time.

Review your attempt with the model answer. If you got the answer wrong, can you see why? Was the problem a lack of knowledge or a failure to understand the question fully?

Fill in the self-assessment box below and decide on your best course of action.

Comfortable with question attempt

↓

Only revisit when comfortable with questions on all topic areas

Not comfortable with question attempts

↓

Focus on these areas by:

- Reworking test your understanding examples in Kaplan's Complete Text
- Revisiting the technical content from Kaplan's pocket notes
- Working any remaining questions on that area in the exam kit

## Stage 3: Final pre-exam revision

We recommend that you **attempt at least one two hour mock examination** containing a set of previously unseen exam standard questions.

It is important that you get a feel for the breadth of coverage of a real exam without advanced knowledge of the topic areas covered – just as you will expect to see on the real exam day.

Ideally this mock should be sat in timed, closed book, real exam conditions and could be:

- a mock examination offered by your tuition provider, and/or
- the pilot paper in the back of this exam kit, and/or
- the practice simulation paper in this kit

Section 1

# PRACTICE QUESTIONS

## THE NATURE AND PURPOSE OF MANAGEMENT ACCOUNTING

1 **Which of the following statements are correct?**

(i) Strategic information is mainly used by senior management in an organisation.

(ii) Productivity measurements are examples of tactical information.

(iii) Operational information is required frequently by its main users.

A (i) and (ii) only

B (i) and (iii) only

C (ii) and (iii) only

D (i), (ii) and (iii)

**(2 marks)**

2 **Reginald is the manager of production department M in a factory which has ten other production departments.**

He receives monthly information that compares planned and actual expenditure for department M. After department M, all production goes into other factory departments to be completed prior to being despatched to customers. Decisions involving capital expenditure in department M are not taken by Reginald.

Which of the following describes Reginald's role in department M?

A A cost centre manager

B An investment centre manager

C A revenue centre manager

**(1 mark)**

3 **Which of the following is NOT CORRECT?**

A Cost accounting can be used for inventory valuation to meet the requirements of internal reporting only.

B Management accounting provides appropriate information for decision making, planning, control and performance evaluation.

C Routine information can be used for both short-term and long-run decisions.

D Financial accounting information can be used for internal reporting purposes.

**(2 marks)**

**4 The following statements relate to financial accounting or to cost and management accounting:**

(i) Financial accounts are historical records.

(ii) Cost accounting is part of financial accounting and establishes costs incurred by an organisation.

(iii) Management accounting is used to aid planning, control and decision making.

Which of the statements are correct?

A (i) and (ii) only

B (i) and (iii) only

C (ii) and (iii) only

D (i), (ii) and (iii)

**(2 marks)**

**5 Which of the following is correct?**

A Qualitative data is generally non-numerical information.

B Information can only be extracted from external sources.

C Operational information gives details of long-term plans only.

**(1 mark)**

**6 The manager of a profit centre is responsible for which of the following?**

(i) Revenues of the centre

(ii) Costs of the centre

(iii) Assets employed in the centre

A (i) only

B (ii) only

C (i) and (ii) only

D (i), (ii) and (iii)

**(2 marks)**

**7 Which of the following would be best described as a short-term tactical plan?**

A Reviewing cost variances and investigate as appropriate

B Comparing actual market share to budget

C Lowering the selling price by 15%

D Monitoring actual sales to budget

**(2 marks)**

**8 The following statements refer to strategic planning:**

(i) It is concerned with quantifiable and qualitative matters.

(ii) It is mainly undertaken by middle management in an organisation.

(iii) It is concerned predominantly with the long term.

Which of the statements are correct?

A (i) and (ii) only

B (i) and (iii) only

C (ii) and (iii) only

D (i), (ii) and (iii)

**(2 marks)**

**9 The following statements relate to responsibility centres:**

(i) Return on capital employed is a suitable measure of performance in both profit and investment centres.

(ii) Cost centres are found in manufacturing organisations but not in service organisations.

(iii) The manager of a revenue centre is responsible for both sales and costs in a part of an organisation.

Which of the statements are incorrect?

A (i) and (ii)

B (ii) and (iii)

C All of them

**(1 mark)**

**10 The following statements refer to qualities of good information:**

(i) It should be communicated to the right person.

(ii) It should always be completely accurate before it is used.

(iii) It should be understandable by the recipient.

Which of the above statements are correct?

A (i) and (ii) only

B (i) and (iii) only

C (ii) and (iii) only

D (i), (ii) and (iii)

**(2 marks)**

**11 A paint manufacturer has a number of departments. Each department is located in a separate building on the same factory site. In the mixing department the basic raw materials are mixed together in very large vessels. These are then moved on to the colour adding department where paints of different colours are created in these vessels. In the next department – the pouring department – the paint is poured from these vessels into litre sized tins. The tins then go on to the labelling department prior to going on to the finished goods department.**

The following statements relate to the paint manufacturer:

(i) The mixing department is a cost centre.

(ii) A suitable cost unit for the colour adding department is a litre tin of paint.

(iii) The pouring department is a profit centre.

Which statement or statements is/are correct?

A (i) only

B (i) and (ii) only

C (i) and (iii) only

D (ii) and (iii) only **(2 marks)**

# TYPES OF COST AND COST BEHAVIOUR

**12 The following diagram represents the behaviour of one element of cost:**

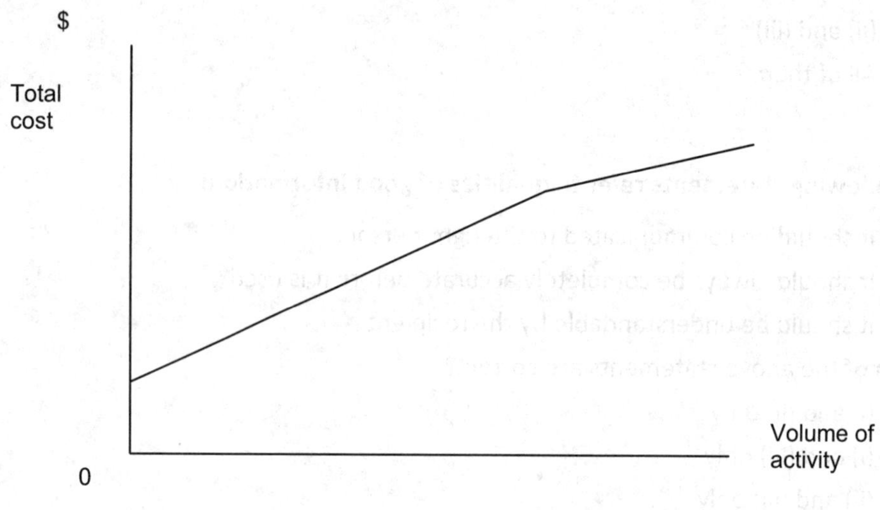


Which one of the following descriptions is consistent with the above diagram?

A Annual total cost of factory power where the supplier sets a tariff based on a fixed charge plus a constant unit cost for consumption which is subject to a maximum annual charge.

B Total annual direct material cost where the supplier charges a constant amount per unit which then reduces to a lower amount per unit after a certain level of purchases.

C Total annual direct material cost where the supplier charges a constant amount per unit but when purchases exceed a certain level a lower amount per unit applies to all purchases in the year.

D Annual total cost of telephone services where the supplier makes a fixed charge and then a constant unit rate for calls up to a certain level. This rate then reduces for all calls above this level. **(2 marks)**

**13 An organisation has the following total costs at three activity levels:**

| Activity level (units) | 8,000 | 12,000 | 15,000 |
|---|---|---|---|
| Total cost | $204,000 | $250,000 | $274,000 |

Variable cost per unit is constant within this activity range and there is a step up of 10% in the total fixed costs when the activity level exceeds 11,000 units.

**What is the total cost at an activity level of 10,000 units?**

A $220,000

B $224,000

C $227,000

D $234,000

**(2 marks)**

**14 A firm has to pay a $0.50 per unit royalty to the inventor of a device which it manufactures and sells.**

The royalty charge would be classified in the firm's accounts as a:

A selling expense

B direct expense

C production overhead

D administrative overhead.

**(2 marks)**

**15 Inventory is valued at total cost per unit.**

Is this statement true or false?

A True

B False

**(1 mark)**

**16 Which of the following is usually classed as a step cost?**

A Supervisor's wages

B Raw materials

C Rates

D Telephone

**(2 marks)**

**17 All of the following may be cost objects except:**

A a cost centre

B a customer

C a manager

D a product.

**(2 marks)**

**18 Depreciation of fixtures is:**

A not a cash cost so is ignored in the cost accounts

B part of manufacturing overheads

C part of prime cost.

**(1 mark)**

**19 Which ONE of the following costs would NOT be classified as a production overhead cost in a food processing company?**

A The cost of renting the factory building

B The salary of the factory manager

C The depreciation of equipment located in the materials store

D The cost of ingredients

**(2 marks)**

**20 The prime cost of a product is the sum of the labour and materials costs that are identifiable to individual units of the product.**

This statement is:

A True

B False

**(1 mark)**

**21 There is to be an increase next year in the rent for a warehouse used to store finished goods ready for sale. The impact of this increase on the value of inventory manufactured next year and held in the warehouse will be:**

A an increase

B a decrease

C no change.

**(1 mark)**

**22 The diagram represents the behaviour of a cost item as the level of output changes:**

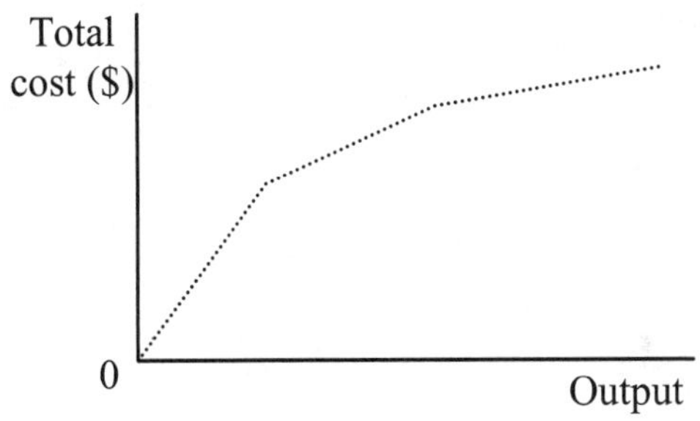


Which ONE of the following situations is described by the graph?

A Discounts are received on additional purchases of material when certain quantities are purchased.

B Employees are paid a guaranteed weekly wage, together with bonuses for higher levels of production.

C A licence is purchased from the government that allows unlimited production.

D Additional space is rented to cope with the need to increase production.

**(2 marks)**

**23 Which ONE of the following would be classified as direct labour?**

A Personnel manager in a company servicing cars

B Bricklayer in a construction company

C General manager in a DIY shop

D Maintenance manager in a company producing cameras

**(2 marks)**

**24 Cost centres are:**

A units of product or service for which costs are ascertained

B amounts of expenditure attributable to various activities

C functions or locations for which costs are ascertained

D a section of an organisation for which budgets are prepared and control exercised.

**(2 marks)**

**25 The following data relate to two output levels of a department:**

| | | |
|---|---|---|
| Machine hours | 17,000 | 18,500 |
| Overheads | \$246,500 | \$251,750 |

The amount of fixed overheads is:

A \$5,250

B \$59,500

C \$187,000

D \$246,500

**(2 marks)**

**26 A kitchen fitting company receives an invoice for sub-contractors who were used to connect the gas supply to a cooker installed in a new kitchen.**

How would this invoice be classified?

A Direct expenses

B Indirect expenses

C Direct labour

D Indirect labour

**(2 marks)**

**27 A manufacturing company has four types of cost (identified as T1, T2 , T3 and T4).**

The total cost for each type at two different production levels is:

| *Cost type* | *Total cost for 125 units* | *Total cost for 180 units* |
|---|---|---|
| | $ | $ |
| T1 | 1,000 | 1,260 |
| T2 | 1,750 | 2,520 |
| T3 | 2,475 | 2,826 |
| T4 | 3,225 | 4,644 |

Which two cost types would be classified as being semi-variable?

A T1 and T3

B T1 and T4

C T2 and T3

D T2 and T4

**(2 marks)**

**28 The following data relate to the overhead expenditure of contract cleaners at two activity levels:**

| | | |
|---|---|---|
| Square metres cleaned | 12,750 | 15,100 |
| Overheads | $73,950 | $83,585 |

Using the high-low method, what is the estimate of the overhead cost if 16,200 square metres are to be cleaned?

A $88,095

B $89,674

C $93,960

D $98,095

**(2 marks)**

**29** **A company manufactures and sells toys and incurs the following three costs:**

(i) Rental of the finished goods warehouse

(ii) Depreciation of its own fleet of delivery vehicles

(iii) Commission paid to sales staff.

**Which of these are classified as distribution costs?**

A (i) and (ii) only

B (ii) and (iii) only

C (ii) and (iii) only.

D (i), (ii) and (iii).

**(2 marks)**

**30** **A company incurs the following costs at various activity levels:**

| *Total cost* | *Activity level* |
|---|---|
| $ | Units |
| 250,000 | 5,000 |
| 312,500 | 7,500 |
| 400,000 | 10,000 |

Using the high-low method what is the variable cost per unit?

A $25

B $30

C $35

D $40

**(2 marks)**

**31** **An organisation manufactures a single product. The total cost of making 4,000 units is $20,000 and the total cost of making 20,000 units is $40,000. Within this range of activity the total fixed costs remain unchanged.**

What is the variable cost per unit of the product?

A $0.80

B $1.20

C $1.25

D $2.00

**(2 marks)**

**32 The following information for advertising and sales revenue has been established over the past six months:**

| *Month* | *Sales revenue* | *Advertising expenditure* |
|---|---|---|
| | $000 | $000 |
| 1 | 155 | 3 |
| 2 | 125 | 2.5 |
| 3 | 200 | 6 |
| 4 | 175 | 5.5 |
| 5 | 150 | 4.5 |
| 6 | 225 | 6.5 |

Using the high-low method, which of the following is the correct equation for linking advertising and sales revenue from the above data?

A Sales revenue = 62,500 + (25 × advertising expenditure)

B Advertising expenditure = –2,500 + (0.04 × sales revenue)

C Sales revenue = 95,000 + (20 × advertising expenditure)

D Advertising expenditure = –4,750 + (0.05 × sales revenue)

**(2 marks)**

**33 A company's weekly costs ($C) were plotted against production level (P) for the last 50 weeks and a regression line calculated to be C = 1,000 +250P. Which statement about the breakdown of weekly costs is true?**

A Weekly fixed costs are $1,000, variable costs per unit are $5.

B Weekly fixed costs are $250, variable costs per unit are $1000.

C Weekly fixed costs are $1,000, variable costs per unit are $250.

D Weekly fixed costs are $20, variable costs per unit are $5.

**(2 marks)**

**34 If a forecasting model based on total cost = fixed cost + variable costs is graphed, the equation is C = F+Vx and the intercept is $7,788. If total costs are $14,520 and x is 3,300 then the value of the slope, to two decimal places, is:**

A 4.40

B 2.04

C –2.04

D 2.36

**(2 marks)**

**35** **The total materials cost of a company is such that when total purchases exceed 15,000 units in any period, then all units purchased, including the first 15,000, are invoiced at a lower cost per unit.**

Determine which of the following graphical representations is consistent with the behaviour of the total materials cost in a period.

A

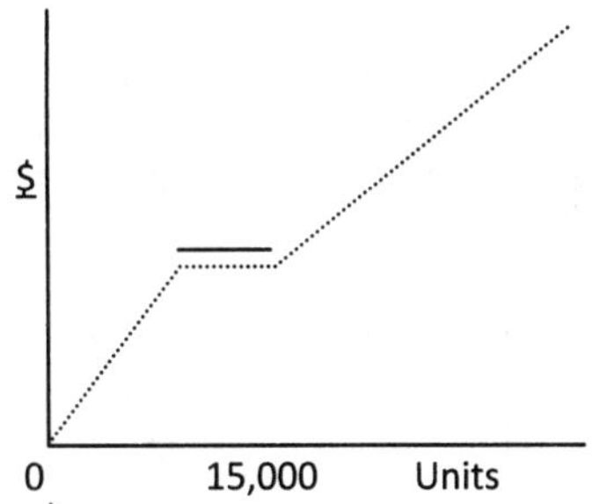


B

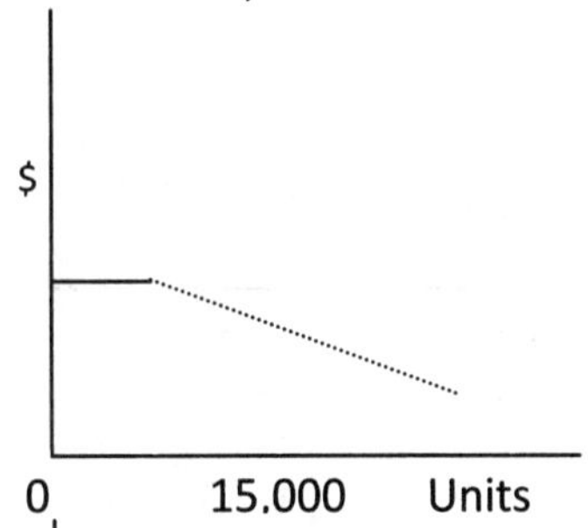


C

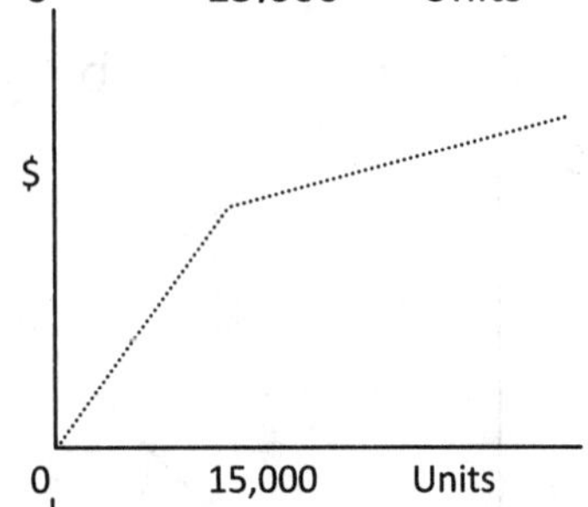


D

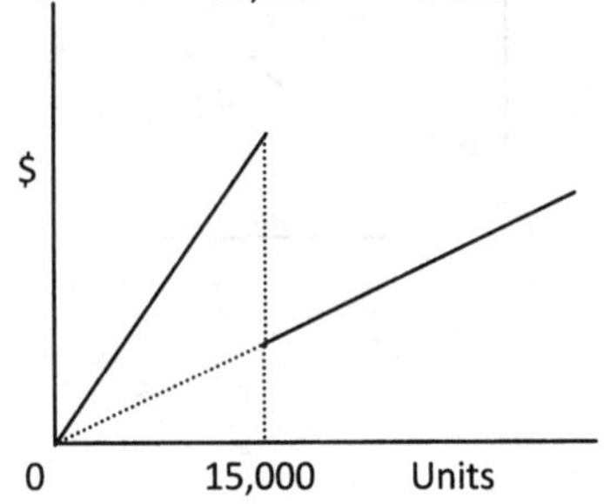


**(2 marks)**

**36** **A supplier of telephone services charges a fixed line rental per period. The first 10 hours of telephone calls by the customer are free, after that all calls are charged at a constant rate per minute up to a maximum, thereafter all calls in the period are again free.**

Which of the following graphs depicts the total cost to the customer of the telephone services in a period?

**A**

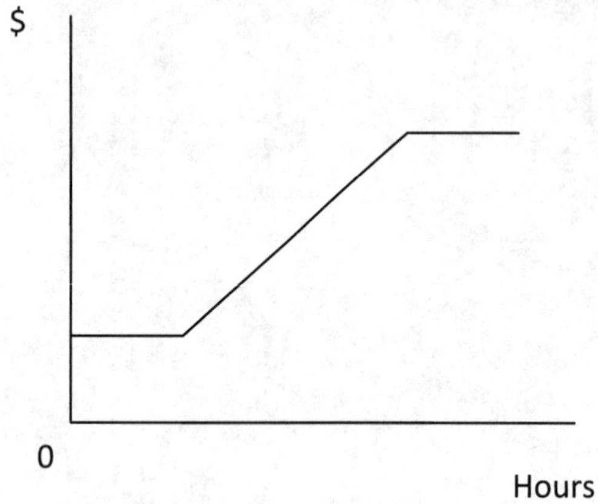


**B**

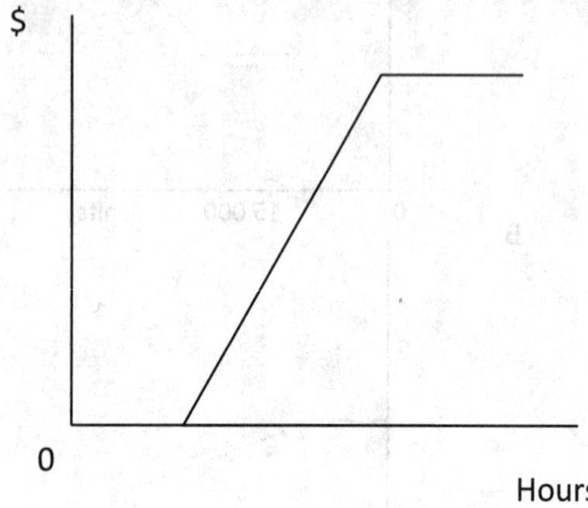


**C**

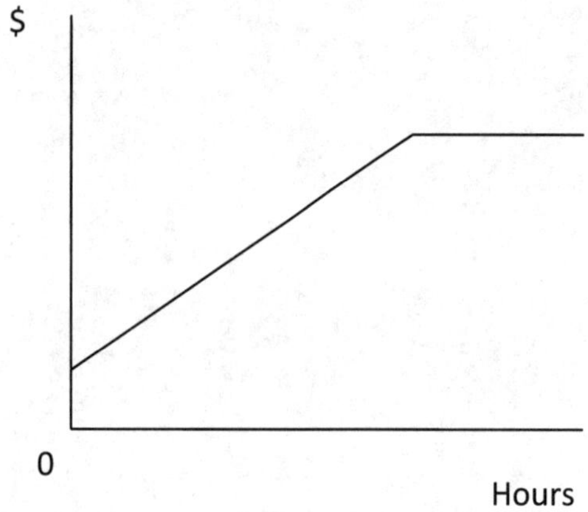


**D**

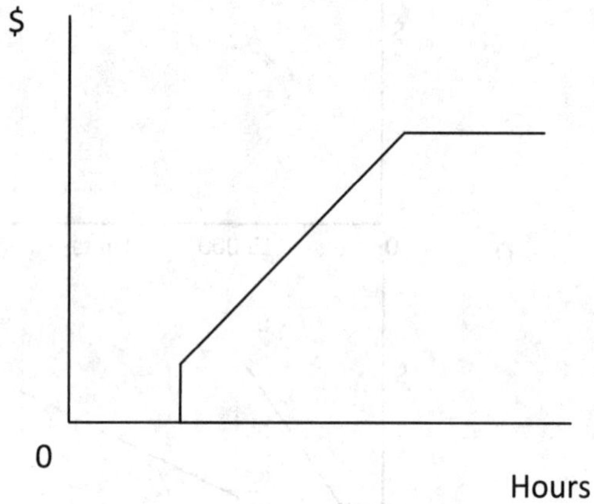


**(2 marks)**

**37 The following production and total cost information relates to a single product organisation for the last three months:**

| *Month* | *Production units* | *Total cost $* |
|---|---|---|
| 1 | 1,200 | 66,600 |
| 2 | 900 | 58,200 |
| 3 | 1,400 | 68,200 |

The variable cost per unit is constant up to a production level of 2,000 units per month but a step up of $6,000 in the monthly total fixed cost occurs when production reaches 1,100 units per month.

What is the total cost for a month when 1,000 units are produced?

A $54,200

B $55,000

C $59,000

D $60,200

**(2 marks)**

## BUSINESS MATHEMATICS

**38 The management of a company is making a decision which could lead to just three possible outcomes – 'high', 'medium' and 'low' levels of demand. Profit and expected value information are as follows :**

| *Outcome* | *Profit* | *Profit × Probability of outcome* |
|---|---|---|
| High | $28,500 | $11,400 |
| Medium | $18,000 | $8,100 |
| Low | $12,000 | $1,800 |

What is the most likely level of profit from making the decision?

A $18,000

B $19,500

C $21,300

D $28,500 **(2 marks)**

**39 The probability of an organisation making a profit of $180,000 next month is half the probability of it making a profit of $75,000.**

**What is the expected profit for next month?**

A $110,000

B $127,000

C $145,000

D $165,000

**(2 marks)**

**40 The management of a company is making a decision which could lead to just three possible outcomes – 'high', 'medium' and 'low' levels of demand. Profit and expected value information are as follows :**

| Outcome | Profit | Profit x probability of outcome |
|---|---|---|
| High | $25,000 | $10,000 |
| Medium | $16,000 | $8,000 |
| Low | $10,000 | $1,000 |

**What is the most likely level of profit from making the decision?**

A $16,000

B $17,000

C $19,000

D $25,000

**(2 marks)**

**41 The correlation coefficient (r) for measuring the connection between two variables (x and y) has been calculated as 0.6.**

How much of the variation in the dependent variable (y) is explained by the variation in the independent variable (x)?

A 36%

B 40%

C 60%

D 64%

**(2 marks)**

**42 A company uses regression analysis to establish its selling overhead costs for budgeting purposes. The data used for the analysis is as follows:**

| *Month* | *Number of salesmen* | *Sales overhead costs* |
|---|---|---|
| | | $000 |
| 1 | 3 | 35.1 |
| 2 | 6 | 46.4 |
| 3 | 4 | 27.0 |
| 4 | 3 | 33.5 |
| 5 | 5 | 41.0 |
| | 21 | 183.0 |

The gradient of the regression line is 4.20. Using regression analysis, what would be the budgeted sales overhead costs for the month, in $000, if there are 5 salesmen employed?

A 28.87

B 39.96

C 41.00

D 56.76

**(2 marks)**

**43 Which of the following are correct with regard to regression analysis?**

(i) In regression analysis the n stands for the number of pairs of data.

(ii) $\Sigma x^2$ is not the same calculation as $(\Sigma x)^2$

(iii) $\Sigma xy$ is calculated by multiplying the total value of x and the total value of y

A (i) and (ii) only

B (i) and (iii) only

C (ii) and (iii) only

D (i), (ii) and (iii)

**(2 marks)**

**44 Regression analysis is being used to find the line of best fit (y = a + bx) from eleven pairs of data. The calculations have produced the following information:**

$\Sigma x = 440$, $\Sigma y = 330$, $\Sigma x^2 = 17{,}986$, $\Sigma y^2 = 10{,}366$ and $\Sigma xy = 13{,}467$

What is the value of 'b' in the equation for the line of best fit (to 2 decimal places)?

A 0.63

B 0.69

C 2.33

D 5.33

**(2 marks)**

**45 An organisation is using linear regression analysis to establish an equation that shows a relationship between advertising expenditure and sales revenue. It will then use the equation to predict sales revenue for given levels of advertising expenditure. Data for the last five periods are as follows:**

| *Period number* | *Advertising expenditure* $000 | *Sales revenue* $000 |
|---|---|---|
| 1 | 17 | 108 |
| 2 | 19 | 116 |
| 3 | 24 | 141 |
| 4 | 22 | 123 |
| 5 | 18 | 112 |

What are the values of '$\Sigma x$', '$\Sigma y$' and 'n' that need to be inserted into the appropriate formula?

| | $\Sigma x$ | $\Sigma y$ | n |
|---|---|---|---|
| A | $600,000 | $100,000 | 5 |
| B | $100,000 | $600,000 | 5 |
| C | $600,000 | $100,000 | 10 |
| D | $100,000 | $600,000 | 10 |

**(2 marks)**

**46 A company has recorded its total cost for different levels of activity over the last five months as follows:**

| *Month* | *Activity level (units)* | *Total cost ($)* |
|---|---|---|
| 7 | 300 | 17,500 |
| 8 | 360 | 19,500 |
| 9 | 400 | 20,500 |
| 10 | 320 | 18,500 |
| 11 | 280 | 17,000 |

The equation for total cost is being calculated using regression analysis on the above data. The equation for total cost is of the general form 'y = a + bx' and the value of 'b' has been calculated correctly as 29.53.

What is the value of 'a' (to the nearest $) in the total cost equation?

A 7,338

B 8,796

C 10,430

D 10,995

**(2 marks)**

**47 Which of the following correlation coefficients indicates the weakest relationship between two variables?**

A + 1.0

B + 0.4

C – 0.6

D – 1.0

**(2 marks)**

**48 A company is deciding which of four products (W, X, Y or Z) to launch. The expected payoff from each of the products is shown below in $000's.**

| Demand | Probability | W | X | Y | Z |
|---|---|---|---|---|---|
| High | 0.5 | 30 | 50 | 40 | 20 |
| Medium | 0.3 | 30 | 0 | 20 | 30 |
| Low | 0.2 | 30 | (50) | 0 | 40 |

If the company wants to maximise the expected profits, which product should be launched?

A W

B X

C Y

D Z

**(2 marks)**

**49 Four sales representatives: A, B, C and D, rate their (independent) chances of achieving certain levels of sales revenue as follows:**

| *Sales representative* | *$40,000* | *$60,000* | *$80,000* |
|---|---|---|---|
| A | 0.3 | 0.4 | 0.3 |
| B | 0.2 | 0.7 | 0.1 |
| C | 0.3 | 0.5 | 0.2 |
| D | 0.3 | 0.3 | 0.4 |

(For example, A rates his chances of selling $40,000 worth of business as 0.3 and B has a 70% chance of selling $60,000 worth.)

On this evidence, the highest expected sales revenue will be from:

A Sales representative A

B Sales representative B

C Sales representative C

D Sales representative D

**(2 marks)**

**50 Connie Furwood estimates the following probabilities of returns on an investment she has made depending on the behaviour of the economy.**

| | *Probability* | *Estimated return %* |
|---|---|---|
| Boom | 0.1 | 13 |
| Normal | 0.65 | 8 |
| Recession | 0.25 | 5 |

What is the expected return on Connie's investment?

A 9.00%

B 8.67%

C 7.75%

D 8.00%

**(2 marks)**

**51 Regression analysis is being used to find the line of best fit (y = a + bx) from five pairs of data. The calculations have produced the following information:**

$\Sigma x = 129$ $\Sigma y = 890$ $\Sigma xy = 23{,}091$ $\Sigma x^2 = 3{,}433$ $\Sigma y^2 = 29{,}929$

What is the value of 'a' in the equation for the line of best fit (to the nearest whole number)?

A 146

B 152

C 210

D 245

**(2 marks)**

**52 Which of the following is a feasible value for a correlation coefficient?**

A +1.2

B 0

C –1.2

D –2.0

**(2 marks)**

## ORDERING AND ACCOUNTING FOR INVENTORY

**53 A manufacturing company uses 28,000 components at an even rate during the year. Each order placed with the supplier of the components is for 1,500 components, which is the economic order quantity. The company holds a buffer inventory of 700 components. The annual cost of holding one component in inventory is €3.**

What is the total annual cost of holding inventory of the component?

A €2,250

B €3,300

C €4,350

D €4,500 **(2 marks)**

**54 The following represent the materials transactions for a company for the month of December 20X6:**

| | $000s |
|---|---|
| Materials purchases | 176 |
| Issued to production | 165 |
| Materials written off | 4 |
| Returned to stores | 9 |
| Returned to suppliers | 8 |

The material inventory at 1 December 20X6 was $15,000.

What is the closing balance on the materials inventory account at 31 December 20X6?

A $5,000

B $16,000

C $23,000

D $31,000

**(2 marks)**

**55 Which of the following statements is correct?**

A A stores ledger account will be updated from a goods received note only.

B A stores requisition will only detail the type of product required by a customer.

C The term 'lead time' is best used to describe the time between receiving an order and paying for it.

D To make an issue from stores authorisation should be required. **(2 marks)**

**56 Perpetual inventory is the counting and valuing of selected items on a rotating basis.**

This statement is:

A True

B False

**(1 mark)**

**57 The double entry for an issue of indirect production materials would be:**

| | | |
|---|---|---|
| A | Dr Materials control account | Cr Finished goods control account |
| B | Dr Production overhead control a/c | Cr Materials control account |
| C | Dr Work-in-progress control account | Cr Production overhead control a/c |
| D | Dr Work-in-progress control account | Cr Materials control account |

**(2 marks)**

**58 Which of the following will be completed by a production department requiring new materials to be obtained from suppliers?**

A A purchase order

B A delivery note

C A purchase requisition

D A goods received note

**(2 marks)**

**59 The following represent transactions on the material account for a company for the month of March 20X8:**

| | $000s |
|---|---|
| Issued to production | 144 |
| Returned to stores | 5 |

The material inventory at 1 March 20X8 was $23,000 and at 31 March 20X8 was $15,000.

How much material was purchased in March 20X8?

A $131,000

B $139,000

C $141,000

D $159,000

**(2 marks)**

**60 Which of the following procedures are carried out to minimise losses from inventory?**

(i) use of standard costs for purchases

(ii) restricted access to stores

(iii) regular stocktaking

A (i) and (ii)

B (ii) and (iii)

C (ii) only

D All of them

**(2 marks)**

# ORDER QUANTITIES AND REORDER LEVELS

**61 A company determines its order quantity for a component using the Economic Order Quantity (EOQ) model.**

What would be the effects on the EOQ and the total annual ordering cost of an increase in the annual cost of holding one unit of the component in inventory?

| | *EOQ* | *Total annual ordering cost* |
|---|---|---|
| A | Lower | Higher |
| B | Higher | Lower |
| C | Lower | No effect |
| D | Higher | No effect |

**(2 marks)**

**62 A company uses the Economic Order Quantity (EOQ) model to establish reorder quantities. The following information relates to the forthcoming period:**

Order costs = \$25 per order

Holding costs = 10% of purchase price = \$4/unit

Annual demand = 20,000 units

Purchase price = \$40 per unit

EOQ = 500 units

No safety inventory is held.

What are the total annual costs of inventory (i.e. the total purchase cost plus total order cost plus total holding cost)?

A \$22,000

B \$33,500

C \$802,000

D \$803,000

**(2 marks)**

**63 Data relating to a particular stores item are as follows:**

| | |
|---|---|
| Average daily usage | 400 units |
| Maximum daily usage | 520 units |
| Minimum daily usage | 180 units |
| Lead time for replenishment of inventory | 10 to 15 days |
| Reorder quantity | 8,000 units |

What is the reorder level (in units) that avoids inventory stockouts?

A 5,000

B 6,000

C 7,800

D 8,000

**(2 marks)**

**64 A large store selling office furniture stocks a popular chair for which the following information is available:**

| | |
|---|---|
| Annual demand: | 4,000 chairs |
| Maximum inventory: | 75 chairs |
| Minimum inventory: | 20 chairs |
| Lead time: | 5 days |
| Re-order quantity: | 100 chairs |

What is the average inventory level?

A 75 chairs

B 70 chairs

C 55 chairs

D 47 chairs

**(2 marks)**

**65 What is the economic batch quantity used to establish?**

Optimal

A reorder quantity

B reorder level

C maximum inventory levels

D quantity to be manufactured.

**(2 marks)**

**66 A company manufactures a product in batches and then holds the items produced in finished goods inventory until they are sold. It is capable of replenishing the product at the rate of 100,000 units/year, but annual sales demand is just 40,000 units. The cost of setting up a batch production run is $1,500 and the cost of holding a unit of the product in inventory is $25/year.**

What is the economic batch quantity for manufacturing this product?

A 2,191 units

B 2,828 units

C 4,472 units

D 10,954 units

**(2 marks)**

**67 Which of the following are included in the cost of holding inventory?**

(i) The cost of insurance

(ii) Rental payments on storage space

(iii) The cost of placing an order

A (i) and (ii)

B (i) and (iii)

C (ii) and (iii)

D (i), (ii) and (iii)

**(2 marks)**

68 **A manufacturing company uses 25,000 components at an even rate during a year. Each order placed with the supplier of the components is for 2,000 components, which is the economic order quantity. The company holds a buffer inventory of 500 components. The annual cost of holding one component in inventory is $2.**

What is the total annual cost of holding inventory of the component?

A $2,000

B $2,500

C $3,000

D $4,000

**(2 marks)**

69 **The purchase price of an inventory item is $42 per unit. In each three-month period the usage of the item is 2,000 units. The annual holding costs associated with one unit is 5% of its purchase price. The EOQ is 185 units.**

What is the cost of placing an order?

A $4.49

B $11.24

C $17.97

D $35.93

**(2 marks)**

---

**The following information applies to questions 70, 71 and 72**

Point uses the economic order quantity (EOQ) model to establish the reorder quantity for raw material Y. The company holds no buffer inventory. Information relating to raw material Y is as follows:

| | |
|---|---|
| Annual usage | 48,000 units |
| Purchase price | $80 per unit |
| Ordering costs | $120 per order |
| Annual holding costs | 10% of the purchase price |

---

70 **The EOQ for raw material Y is:**

A 438

B 800

C 1,200

D 3,795

**(2 marks)**

71 **The total annual cost of purchasing, ordering and holding inventory of raw material Y is:**

A $3,849,600

B $3,850,400

C $3,853,600

D $3,854,400

**(2 marks)**

**72 The supplier has offered Point a discount of 1% on the purchase price if each order placed is for 2,000 units.**

The total annual saving to Point of accepting this offer is:

A $29,280

B $30,080

C $37,200

D $38,000 **(2 marks)**

**73 A company uses components at the rate of 600 units per month, which are bought in at a cost of $2.24 each from the supplier. It costs $8.75 each time to place an order, regardless of the quantity ordered. The supplier offers a 5% discount on the purchase price for order quantities of 2,000 items or more. The current EOQ is 750 units. The total holding cost is 10% per annum of the value of inventory held.**

What is the change in total cost to the company of moving to an order quantity of 2,000 units?

A $601 additional cost

B $730 additional cost

C $730 saving

D $601 saving

**(2 marks)**

**74 A company makes a component for one of its products in-house. It uses an average of 5,000 of these throughout the year. The production rate for these components is 500 per week and the cost of holding one item for the year is $1.50. The factory is open for 50 weeks per year. The company has calculated that the economic batch quantity is 2,000. What is the production setup cost per batch?**

A $213

B $240

C $480

D $960

**(2 marks)**

# ACCOUNTING FOR LABOUR

**75 The following statements relate to labour costs:**

There would be an increase in the total cost for labour as a result of:

(i) additional labour being employed on a temporary basis

(ii) a department with spare capacity being made to work more hours

(iii) a department which is at full capacity switching from the production of one product to another.

Which of the above is/are correct?

A (i) only

B (ii) only

C (iii) only

D (i) and (iii) only

**(2 marks)**

**76 A manufacturing firm is very busy and overtime is being worked.**

The amount of overtime premium contained in direct wages would normally be classed as:

A part of prime cost

B factory overheads

C direct labour costs

D administrative overheads.

**(2 marks)**

**77 KL currently pays its direct production workers on a time basis at a rate of $6.50 per hour. In an effort to improve productivity, the company is introducing a bonus based on (time taken/time allowed) × time saved × rate per hour. The standard time allowed for a worker in the Assembly Department to perform this particular operation once has been agreed at 37.5 minutes.**

In the first week of the scheme's operation, one employee worked for a total of 44 hours and performed 94 operations.

The gross wages for this employee based on a time rate of $6.50 per hour plus the productivity bonus based on (time taken/time allowed) × time saved × rate per hour, to 2 decimal places, is:

A $214.20

B $357.80

C $381.88

D $977.60

**(2 marks)**

**78 If the direct labour costs in a manufacturing company are $95,000 in March, the costs would be recorded in the cost ledger as:**

A Debit Work-in-progress $95,000, Credit Wages and salaries $95,000

B Debit Wages and salaries $95,000, Credit Bank $95,000

C Debit Wages and salaries $95,000, Credit Work-in-progress $95,000

D Debit Bank $95,000, Credit Wages and salaries $95,000

**(2 marks)**

**79 Budgeted production in a factory for next period is 4,800 units. Each unit requires five labour hours to make. Labour is paid $10 per hour. Idle time represents 20% of the total labour time.**

**What is the budgeted total labour cost for the next period?**

A $192,000

B $240,000

C $288,000

D $300,000

**(2 marks)**

**80** **The following statements refer to situations occurring in Process Q of an organisation which operates a series of consecutive processes:**

(i) Direct labour is working at below the agreed productivity level.

(ii) A machine breakdown has occurred.

(iii) Direct labour is waiting for work to be completed in a previous process.

Which of these situations could give rise to idle time?

A (i) and (ii) only

B (i) and (iii) only

C (ii) and (iii) only

D (i), (ii) and (iii)

**(2 marks)**

**81** **A direct labour employee works a standard 37 hour week and is paid a basic rate of $15 per hour. Overtime is paid at time and a half. In a week when 40 hours were worked and a bonus of $20 was paid, what was the direct labour cost?**

A $555

B $600

C $622.50

D $642.50

**(2 marks)**

**82** **At 1 January a company employed 5,250 employees. Due to expansion the number of employees increased to 5,680 by 31 December. During the year 360 staff left the company and were replaced. What was the labour turnover rate?**

A 6.3%

B 6.6%

C 6.9%

D 360 staff

**(2 marks)**

---

**The following information applies to questions 83, 84 and 85**

A company records the following information concerning a product:

| | |
|---|---|
| Standard time allowed per unit | 16 minutes |
| Actual output in period | 720 units |
| Actual hours worked | 180 |
| Budgeted hours | 185 |

---

**83** **What is the labour efficiency ratio?**

A 93.75%

B 97.3%

C 102.5%

D 106.7%

**(2 marks)**

**84 What is the labour capacity ratio?**

A 102.8%

B 99.4%

C 98.6%

D 97.3%

**(2 marks)**

**85 What is the production volume ratio?**

A 97.3%

B 102.5%

C 103.8%

D 106.7%

**(2 marks)**

# ACCOUNTING FOR OVERHEADS

**86 A factory consists of two production cost centres (G and H) and two service cost centres (J and K). The total overheads allocated and apportioned to each centre are as follows:**

| *G* | *H* | *J* | *K* |
|---|---|---|---|
| $40,000 | $50,000 | $30,000 | $18,000 |

The work done by the service cost centres can be represented as follows:

| | G | H | J | K |
|---|---|---|---|---|
| Percentage of service cost centre J to | 30% | 70% | – | – |
| Percentage of service cost centre K to | 50% | 40% | 10% | – |

The company apportions service cost centre costs to production cost centres using a method that fully recognises any work done by one service cost centre for another.

What are the total overheads for production cost centre G after the reapportionment of all service cost centre costs?

A $58,000

B $58,540

C $59,000

D $59,540

**(2 marks)**

**87 An overhead absorption rate is used to:**

A share out common costs over benefiting cost centres

B find the total overheads for a cost centre

C charge overheads to products

D control overheads.

**(2 marks)**

**88 A factory consists of two production cost centres (P and Q) and two service cost centres (X and Y). The total allocated and apportioned overhead for each is as follows:**

| *P* | *Q* | *X* | *Y* |
|---|---|---|---|
| $95,000 | $82,000 | $46,000 | $30,000 |

It has been estimated that each service cost centre does work for the other cost centres in the following proportions:

| | *P* | *Q* | *X* | *Y* |
|---|---|---|---|---|
| Percentage of service cost centre X to | 40 | 40 | – | 20 |
| Percentage of service cost centre Y to | 30 | 60 | 10 | – |

After the reapportionment of service cost centre costs has been carried out using a method that fully recognises the reciprocal service arrangements in the factory, what is the total overhead for production cost centre P?

A $122,400

B $124,716

C $126,000

D $127,000

**(2 marks)**

**89 A cost centre has an overhead absorption rate of $4.25 per machine hour, based on a budgeted activity level of 12,400 machine hours.**

In the period covered by the budget, actual machine hours worked were 2% more than the budgeted hours and the actual overhead expenditure incurred in the cost centre was $56,389.

What was the total over or under absorption of overheads in the cost centre for the period?

A $1,054 over absorbed

B $2,635 under absorbed

C $3,689 over absorbed

D $3,689 under absorbed

**(2 marks)**

**90 Over-absorbed overheads occur when:**

A absorbed overheads exceed actual overheads

B absorbed overheads exceed budgeted overheads

C actual overheads exceed budgeted overheads

D budgeted overheads exceed absorbed overheads.

**(2 marks)**

**91 The management accountant's report shows that fixed production overheads were over-absorbed in the last accounting period. The combination that is certain to lead to this situation is:**

A production volume is lower than budget and actual expenditure is higher than budget

B production volume is higher than budget and actual expenditure is higher than budget

C production volume and actual cost are as budgeted

D production volume is higher than budget and actual expenditure is lower than budget.

**(2 marks)**

**92 At the end of a period, in an integrated cost and financial accounting system, the accounting entries for $10,000 overheads over-absorbed would be:**

| | | | | |
|---|---|---|---|---|
| A | Dr | Work-in-progress control account | Cr | Overhead control account |
| B | Dr | Income statement | Cr | Work-in-progress control account |
| C | Dr | Income statement | Cr | Overhead control account |
| D | Dr | Overhead control account | Cr | Income statement |

**(2 marks)**

**93 During a period $50,000 was incurred for indirect labour. In a typical cost ledger, the double entry for this is:**

| | | | | |
|---|---|---|---|---|
| A | Dr | Wages control | Cr | Overhead control |
| B | Dr | WIP control | Cr | Wages control |
| C | Dr | Overhead control | Cr | Wages control |
| D | Dr | Wages control | Cr | WIP control |

**(2 marks)**

**94 Iddon makes two products, Pye and Tan, in a factory divided into two production departments, machining and assembly. In order to find a fixed overhead cost per unit, the following budgeted data are relevant.**

| | *Machining* | *Assembly* |
|---|---|---|
| Direct and allocated fixed costs | $120,000 | $72,000 |
| Labour hours per unit | | |
| Pye | 0.50 hour | 0.20 hour |
| Tan | 1.00 hour | 0.25 hour |

Budgeted production is 4,000 units of each product (8,000 units in all) and fixed overheads are to be absorbed by reference to labour hours.

What is the budgeted fixed overhead cost of a unit of Pye?

A $18

B $20

C $24

D $28

**(2 marks)**

**95 What is cost apportionment?**

A The charging of discrete identifiable items of cost to cost centres or cost units.

B The collection of costs attributable to cost centres and cost units using the costing methods, principles and techniques prescribed for a particular business entity.

C The process of establishing the costs of cost centres or cost units.

D The division of costs amongst two or more cost centres in proportion to the estimated benefit received, using a proxy, e.g. square feet.

**(2 marks)**

**96 A law firm recovers overheads on chargeable consulting hours. Budgeted overheads were $615,000 and actual consulting hours were 32,150. Overheads were under-recovered by $35,000.**

If actual overheads were $694,075, the budgeted overhead absorption rate per hour is (to 2 decimal places):

A $20.21

B $20.50

C $21.59

D $22.68

**(2 marks)**

**97 A finishing department absorbs production overheads using a direct labour hour basis. Budgeted production overheads for the year just ended were $268,800 for the department, and actual production overhead costs were $245,600.**

If actual labour hours worked were 45,000 and production overheads were over-absorbed by $6,400, what was the overhead absorption rate per labour hour?

A $5.32

B $5.60

C $5.83

D $6.12

**(2 marks)**

**98 A firm absorbs overheads on labour hours. In one period 11,500 hours were worked, actual overheads were $138,000 and there was $23,000 over-absorption. The overhead absorption rate per hour was:**

A $10

B $12

C $13

D $14

**(2 marks)**

**99 A factory has two production departments, X and Y, and two service departments C and D.**

**The following information costs relates to the overhead costs in each department.**

| | *Manufacturing departments* | | *Service departments* | |
|---|---|---|---|---|
| | X | Y | C | D |
| Overhead costs | $5,000 | $7,500 | $3,200 | $4,600 |
| Proportion of usage of services of C | 50% | 40% | – | 10% |
| Proportion of usage of services of D | 20% | 60% | 20% | – |

Using the reciprocal method of apportioning service department costs, the total overhead costs allocated to department X will be:

A $5,000

B $7,520

C $8,105

D $12,195

**(2 marks)**

**100 The following budgeted and actual results relate to production activity and overhead costs in WX.**

| | BUDGET | ACTUAL |
|---|---|---|
| Production overhead costs | | |
| Fixed | $36,000 | $39,000 |
| Variable | $9,000 | $12,000 |
| Direct labour hours worked | 18,000 hours | 20,000 hours |

An absorption costing system is used and production overhead costs are absorbed into output costs on a direct labour hour basis.

The total production overhead (both fixed and variable) during the period was:

A over-absorbed by $1,000

B under-absorbed by $1,000

C under-absorbed by $5,000

D under-absorbed by $6,000.

**(2 marks)**

**101 Lerna produces hydras in three production departments and needs to apportion budgeted monthly fixed costs between those departments. Budgeted costs are as follows:**

| | $ |
|---|---|
| Rent | 2,000 |
| Rates | 1,000 |
| Plant insurance | 1,000 |
| Plant depreciation | 10,000 |
| Supervisor's salary | 7,000 |
| | 21,000 |

The following additional information is available.

| | *Department A* | *Department B* | *Department C* |
|---|---|---|---|
| Area (square feet) | 3,800 | 3,500 | 700 |
| Value of machinery ($000) | 210 | 110 | 80 |
| Number of employees | 34 | 16 | 20 |

The total budgeted monthly fixed overhead cost for Department C is:

A $1,837.50

B $4,462.50

C $7,000.00

D $10,600.00

**(2 marks)**

**102 The following information is available regarding the fixed overhead costs and output of the two production departments of a firm.**

| *Department* | *S* | *T* |
|---|---|---|
| Allocated or apportioned fixed overhead | $60,000 | $100,000 |
| Total cost of direct materials used | $120,000 | $100,000 |
| Total productive labour hours | 5,000 | 10,000 |

A particular product has the following variable cost.

| | | | | $ |
|---|---|---|---|---|
| Materials | | | | |
| Department S | 3 kg | @ | $4 per kg | 12 |
| Department T | 2 kg | @ | $4 per kg | 8 |
| Labour | | | | |
| Department S | ½ hour | @ | $10 per hour | 5 |
| Department T | 1½ hours | @ | $10 per hour | 15 |
| Variable overheads | 1 hour | @ | $5 per hour | 5 |
| | | | | 45 |

If fixed overheads are absorbed on the basis of departmental material cost, the fixed overhead cost per unit is:

A $5.50

B $12.00

C $14.00

D $21.00

**(2 marks)**

# MARGINAL AND ABSORPTION COSTING

**103 PQR sells one product. The cost card for that product is given below:**

| | $ |
|---|---|
| Direct materials | 4 |
| Direct labour | 5 |
| Variable production overhead | 3 |
| Fixed production overhead | 2 |
| Variable selling cost | 3 |

The selling price per unit is $20. Budgeted fixed overheads are based on budgeted production of 1,000 units. Opening inventory was 200 units and closing inventory was 150 units. Sales during the period were 800 units and actual fixed overheads incurred were $1,500.

The total contribution earned during the period was:

A $2000

B $2,500

C $4,000

D $2,500 **(2 marks)**

**104 The following diagram represents a profit/volume chart for an organisation:**

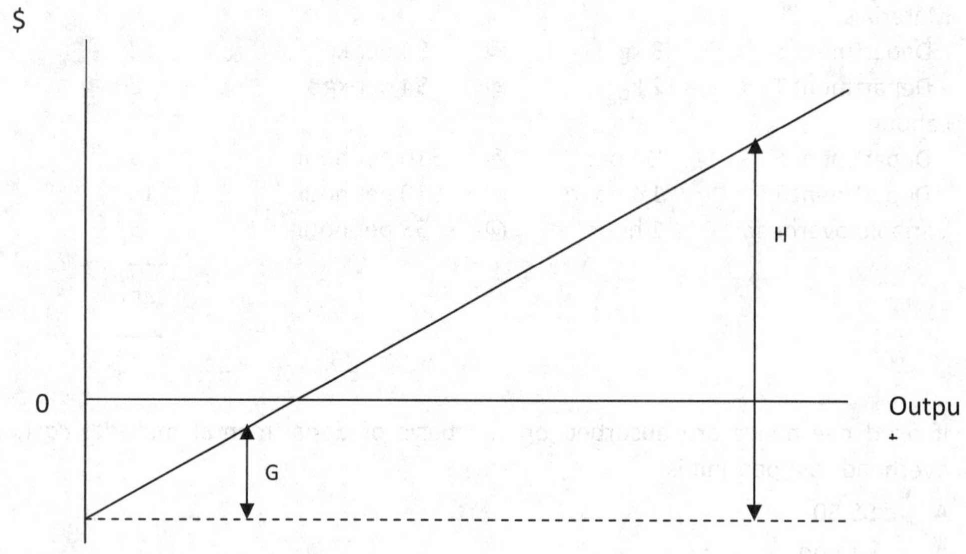


At the specific levels indicated what do the lines 'G' and 'H' represent?

| | Line 'G' | Line 'H' |
|---|---|---|
| A | Loss | Profit |
| B | Loss | Contribution |
| C | Contribution | Profit |
| D | Contribution | Contribution |

**(2 marks)**

**105 An organisation manufactures and sells a single product that has a variable cost of $24 per unit and a contribution to sales ratio of 40%. Total monthly fixed costs are $720,000.**

What is the monthly breakeven point (in units)?

A 18,000

B 20,000

C 30,000

D 45,000 **(2 marks)**

**106 E operates a marginal costing system. For the forthcoming year, variable costs are budgeted to be 60% of sales value and fixed costs are budgeted to be 10% of sales value.**

If E increases its selling prices by 10%, but if fixed costs, variable costs per unit and sales volume remain unchanged, the effect on E's contribution would be:

A a decrease of 2%

B an increase of 5%

C an increase of 10%

D an increase of 25%.

**(2 marks)**

**107 Last month a manufacturing company's profit was $2,000, calculated using absorption costing principles. If marginal costing principles had been used, a loss of $3,000 would have occurred. The company's fixed production cost is $2 per unit. Sales last month were 10,000 units.**

What was last month's production (in units)?

A 7,500

B 9,500

C 10,500

D 12,500

**(2 marks)**

**108 A company produces and sells a single product whose variable cost is $6 per unit.**

Fixed costs have been absorbed over the normal level of activity of 200,000 units and have been calculated as $2 per unit.

The current selling price is $10 per unit.

How much profit is made under marginal costing if the company sells 250,000 units?

A $500,000

B $600,000

C $900,000

D $1,000,000 **(2 marks)**

**109 A company manufactures and sells a single product. For this month the budgeted fixed production overheads are $48,000, budgeted production is 12,000 units and budgeted sales are 11,720 units.**

The company currently uses absorption costing.

If the company used marginal costing principles instead of absorption costing for this month, what would be the effect on the budgeted profit?

A $1,120 higher

B $1,120 lower

C $3,920 higher

D $3,920 lower

**(2 marks)**

**110 When opening inventory was 8,500 litres and closing inventory was 6,750 litres, a firm had a profit of $62,100 using marginal costing.**

Assuming that the fixed overhead absorption rate was $3 per litre, what would be the profit using absorption costing?

A $41,850

B $56,850

C $67,350

D $82,350

**(2 marks)**

**111 A company has established a marginal costing profit of $72,300. Opening inventory was 300 units and closing inventory is 750 units. The fixed production overhead absorption rate has been calculated as $5/unit.**

What was the profit under absorption costing?

A $67,050

B $70,050

C $74,550

D $77,550

**(2 marks)**

**The following data are for questions 112 and 113**

The budget for Bright's first month of trading, producing and selling boats was as follows:

| | $000 |
|---|---|
| Variable production cost of boats | 45 |
| Fixed production costs | 30 |
| Production costs of 750 boats | 75 |
| Closing inventory of 250 boats | (25) |
| Production cost of 500 sold | 50 |
| Variable selling costs | 5 |
| Fixed selling costs | 25 |
| | 80 |
| Profit | 10 |
| Sales revenue | 90 |

The budget has been produced using an absorption costing system.

**112 If a marginal costing system were used, the budgeted profit would be:**

A $22,500 lower

B $10,000 lower

C $10,000 higher

D $22,500 higher

**(2 marks)**

**113 Assume that at the end of the first month unit variable costs and fixed costs and selling price for the month were in line with the budget and any inventory was valued at the same unit cost as in the above budget.**

However, if production was actually 700 and sales 600, what would be the reported profit using absorption costing?

A $9,000

B $12,000

C $14,000

D $15,000

**(2 marks)**

**114 Which of the following are true of marginal costing?**

(i) The marginal cost of a product includes an allowance for fixed production costs.

(ii) The marginal cost of a product represents the additional cost of producing an extra unit.

(iii) If the inventory increases over a year, the profits under absorption costing will be lower than with marginal costing.

A (i) only

B (ii) only

C (ii) and (iii) only

D (i), (ii) and (iii)

**(2 marks)**

**115 A breakeven chart for a company is depicted as follows:**

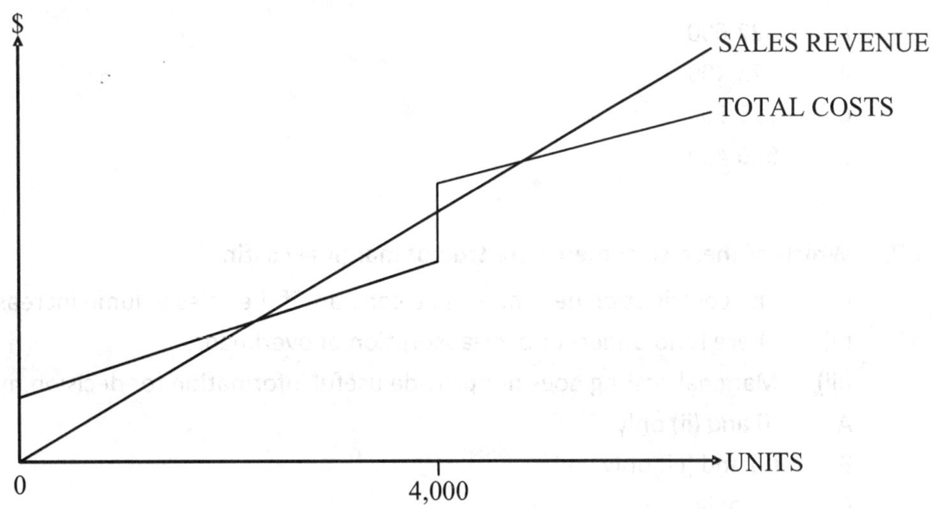

Which one of the following statements is consistent with the above chart?

A Both selling price per unit and variable cost per unit are constant.

B Selling price per unit is constant but variable cost per unit increases for sales over 4,000 units.

C Variable cost per unit is constant but the selling price per unit increases for sales over 4,000 units.

D Selling price per unit increases for sales over 4,000 units and there is an increase in the total fixed costs at 4,000 units.

**(2 marks)**

**116 An organisation manufactures and sells a single product. At the budgeted level of output of 2,400 units per week, the unit cost and selling price structure is as follows:**

| | *$ per unit* | *$ per unit* |
|---|---|---|
| Selling price | | 60 |
| Less – variable production cost | 15 | |
| – other variable cost | 5 | |
| – fixed cost | 30 | |
| | | (50) |
| Profit | | 10 |

What is the breakeven point (in units per week)?

A 1,200

B 1,600

C 1,800

D 2,400

**(2 marks)**

**117 A new company has set up a marginal costing system and has a budgeted contribution for the period of $26,000 based on sales of 13,000 units and production of 15,000 units. This level of production represents the firm's expected long-term level of production. The company's budgeted fixed production costs are $3,000 for the period.**

If the company were to change to an absorption costing system the budgeted profit would be:

A $22,600

B $23,400

C $25,600

D $26,400

**(2 marks)**

**118 Which of these statements are true of marginal costing?**

(i) The contribution per unit will be constant if the sales volume increases.

(ii) There is no under- or over-absorption of overheads.

(iii) Marginal costing does not provide useful information for decision making.

A (i) and (ii) only

B (ii) and (iii) only

C (ii) only

D (i), (ii) and (iii)

**(2 marks)**

**119** **A company that makes and sells a single product has budgeted the following unit costs and profit.**

| | $ |
|---|---|
| Sales price | 8 |
| Variable cost | 3 |
| Fixed cost | 4 |
| | — |
| Profit | 1 |
| | — |

The budgeted profit is $125,000.

What is the margin of safety expressed as a percentage of budgeted sales?

A 15%

B 17.5%

C 20%

D 25%

**(2 marks)**

**120** **The profit-volume chart for a single product company is as follows :**

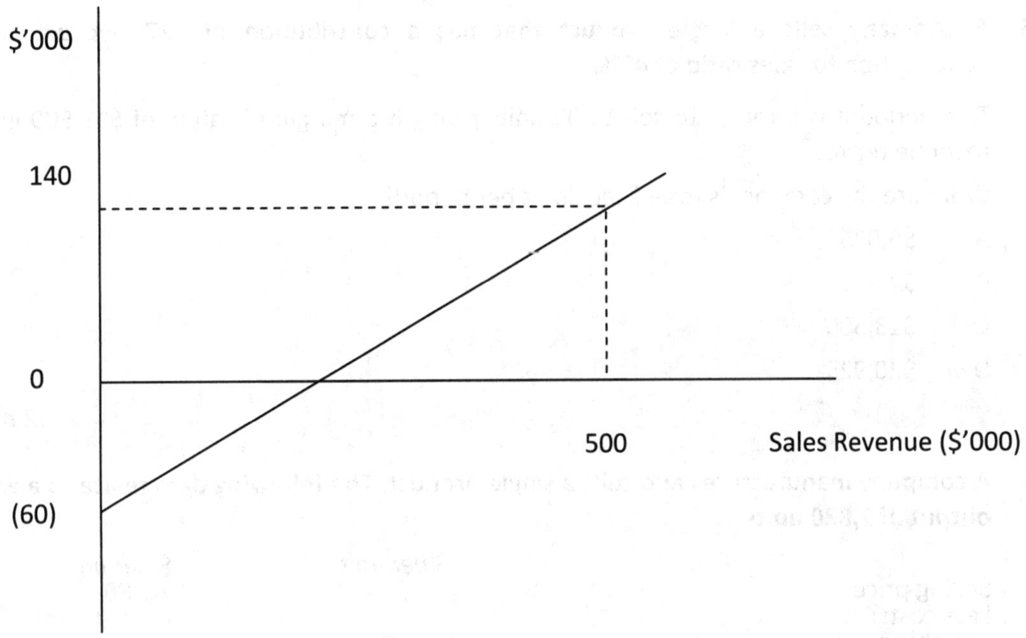


What is the product's contribution to sales ratio (expressed as a %)?

A 16%

B 28%

C 40%

D 72%

**(2 marks)**

**121 In a period, a company had opening inventory of 31,000 units of Product G and closing inventory of 34,000 units. Profits based on marginal costing were $850,500 and profits based on absorption costing were $955,500.**

If the budgeted fixed costs for the company for the period were $1,837,500, what was the budgeted level of activity?

A 24,300 units

B 27,300 units

C 52,500 units

D 65,000 units

**(2 marks)**

**122 The unit price of a product is higher than its variable cost of manufacture and sale. If both the selling price per unit and variable cost per unit rise by 10%, the breakeven point will:**

A remain constant

B increase

C fall

D be impossible to determine without further information.

**(2 marks)**

**123 A company sells a single product that has a contribution of $27 per unit and a contribution to sales ratio of 45%.**

This period it is forecast to sell 1,000 units giving it a margin of safety of $13,500 in sales revenue terms.

What are the company's total fixed costs per period?

A $6,075

B $7,425

C $13,500

D $20,925

**(2 marks)**

**124 A company manufactures and sells a single product. The following data relate to a weekly output of 2,880 units:**

| | *$ per unit* | *$ per unit* |
|---|---|---|
| Selling price | | 80 |
| Less costs: | | |
| Variable production | 30 | |
| Other variable | 10 | |
| Fixed | 25 | |
| | | (65) |
| Profit | | 15 |

What is the weekly breakeven point (in units)?

A 1,900

B 1,440

C 1,800

D 4,800

**(2 marks)**

**125 AL makes a single product that it sells for $10 per unit. Fixed costs are $48,000 per month and the product has a contribution to sales ratio of 40%.**

In a period when actual sales revenue was $140,000, AL's margin of safety, in units, was:

A 2,000

B 6,000

C 8,000

D 14,000

**126 An organisation manufactures a single product that is sold for $60 per unit. The organisation's total monthly fixed costs are $54,000 and it has a contribution to sales ratio of 40%. This month it plans to manufacture and sell 4,000 units.**

What is the organisation's margin of safety this month (in units)?

A 1,500

B 1,750

C 2,250

D 2,500

**(2 marks)**

**127 The following breakeven chart has been drawn showing lines for total cost (TC), total variable cost (TVC), total fixed cost (TFC) and total sales revenue (TSR):**

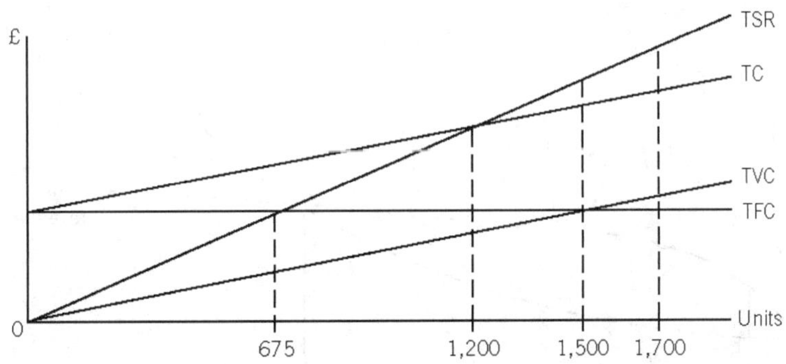


If fixed costs are $3,000, what is the total contribution at the 1,700 units level of activity?

A $7,556

B $4,250

C $3,400

D $1,700 **(2 marks)**

**128 Dane makes and sells a single product which has a selling price of $26, prime costs are $10 and overheads (all fixed) are absorbed at 50% of prime cost. Fixed overheads are $50,000.**

What is the breakeven point (to the nearest whole unit)?

A 1,923

B 3,125

C 4,545

D 5,000 **(2 marks)**

**129 A company has calculated its margin of safety as 20% on budgeted sales and budgeted sales are 5,000 units per month.**

What would be the budgeted fixed costs if the budgeted contribution was $25 per unit?

A $100,000

B $125,000

C $150,000

D $160,000

**(2 marks)**

**130 In a given period, the production level of an item exactly matches the level of sales. The profit reported will be identical whether marginal or absorption costing is used.**

This statement is:

A True

B False

**(1 mark)**

**131 Consider the following graph for total costs and total revenue:**

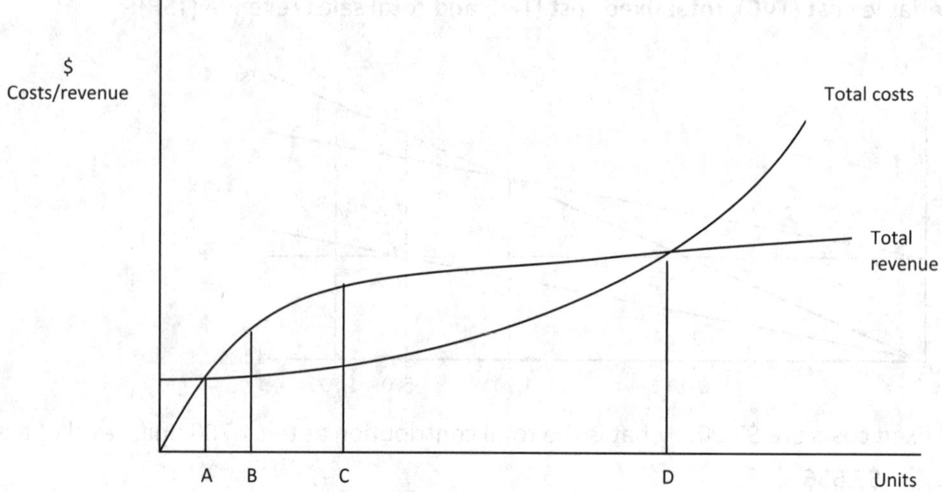


At which point on the above graph is it most likely that profits will be maximised?

A

B

C

D

**(2 marks)**

**132 Four lines representing expected costs and revenues have been drawn on a breakeven chart:**

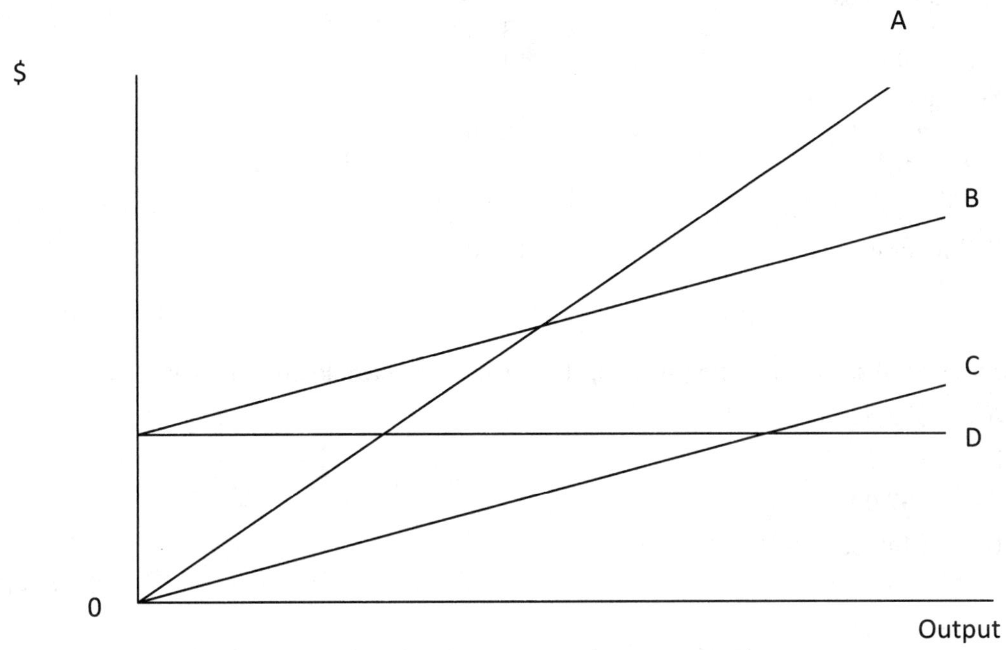


Which line represents total variable cost?

A Line A

B Line B

C Line C

D Line D

**(2 marks)**

**133 For a product that has a positive unit contribution, which of the following events would tend to increase total contribution by the greatest amount?**

A 10% decrease in variable cost.

B 10% increase in selling price.

C 10% increase in volume sold.

D 15% decrease in total fixed costs.

**134 Exp has compiled the following standard cost card for its main product.**

| | $ |
|---|---|
| Production costs | |
| Fixed | 33.00 |
| Variable | 45.10 |
| Selling costs | |
| Fixed | 64.00 |
| Variable | 7.20 |
| Profit | 14.70 |
| Selling price | 164.00 |

Under an absorption costing system, closing inventory would be valued at:

A $52.30

B $78.10

C $97.00

D $149.30

**(2 marks)**

**135 Four lines have been labelled as J, K, L and M at different levels of output on the following profit/volume chart:**

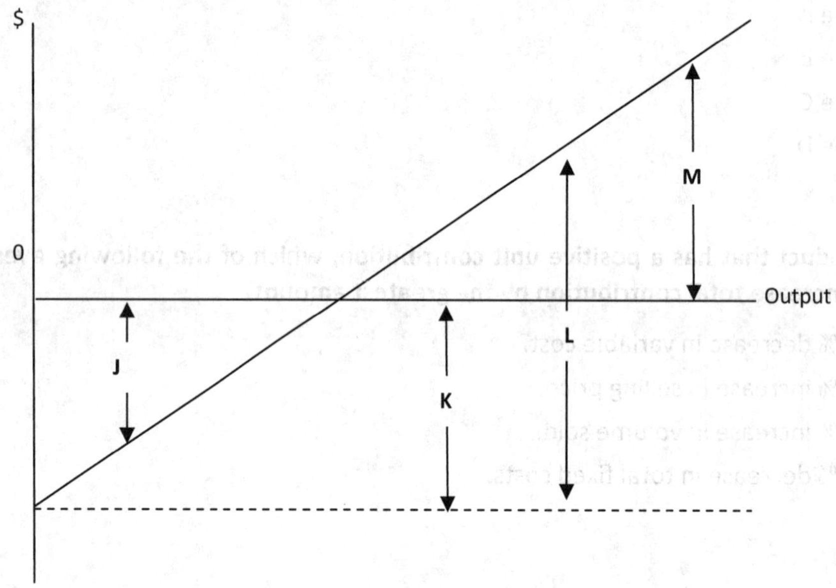


Which line represents the total contribution at the corresponding level of output?

A Line J

B Line K

C Line L

D Line M

**(2 marks)**

**136 A company manufactures a single product that it sells for $15 per unit. The product has a contribution to sales ratio of 40%. The company's weekly breakeven point is sales of $18,000.**

What would be the profit in a week when 1,500 units are sold?

A $900

B $1,800

C $2,700

D $4,500

**(2 marks)**

**137 A company has the following budgeted information for the coming month:**

| | |
|---|---|
| Budgeted sales revenue | $500,000 |
| Budgeted contribution | $200,000 |
| Budgeted profit | $50,000 |

What is the budgeted breakeven sales revenue?

A $125,000

B $350,000

C $375,000

D $450,000

**(2 marks)**

# RELEVANT COSTING

**138 In a short-term decision-making context, which ONE of the following would be a relevant cost?**

A Specific development costs already incurred.

B The cost of special material which will be purchased.

C Depreciation on existing equipment.

D The original cost of raw materials currently in inventory that will be used on the project.

**(2 marks)**

**139 The following statements relate to relevant cost concepts in decision making:**

(i) Materials can never have an opportunity cost whereas labour can.

(ii) The annual depreciation charge is not a relevant cost.

(iii) Fixed costs would have a relevant cost element if a decision causes a change in their total expenditure.

Which statements are correct?

A (i) and (ii) only

B (ii) and (iii) only

C (i), (ii) and (iii)

**(1 mark)**

**140 A contract is under consideration that requires 400 labour hours to complete. There are 150 hours of spare labour capacity.**

The remaining hours for the contract can be found either by weekend overtime working paid at double the normal rate of pay or by diverting labour from the manufacture of product QZ. If the contract is undertaken and labour is diverted, then sales of product QZ will be lost. Product QZ takes three labour hours per unit to manufacture and makes a contribution of $12 per unit. The normal rate of pay for labour is $9 per hour.

What is the total relevant cost of labour for the contract?

A $3,250

B $3,600

C $4,500

D $4,600

**(2 marks)**

**141 A company purchased a machine four years ago at a cost of $25,000. It is to be depreciated on a straight line basis over five years.**

It is no longer used on normal production work and has a scrap value of $2,000.

A one-off contract is being considered which would make use of this machine for six months. The contract would require adjustments to be made to the machine costing $800. At the end of the contract it is estimated that the scrap value would be $1,500.

What is the relevant cost of the machine to the contract?

A $1,300

B $3,300

C $4,300

D $23,500

**(2 marks)**

**142 A company has an asset that originally cost $58,000, but would now cost just $37,000 to replace. The asset could be sold for scrap to earn $11,000. Alternatively, it could be used in a small project that would earn net income of $17,500. The asset has no other use.**

What is the relevant value of the asset?

A $6,500

B $11,000

C $17,500

D $37,000

**(2 marks)**

**143 A company has just secured a new contract that requires 500 hours of labour.**

There are 400 hours of spare labour capacity. The remaining hours could be worked as overtime at time-and-a-half or labour could be diverted from the production of product X. Product X currently earns a contribution of $4 in two labour hours and direct labour is currently paid at a rate of $12 per normal hour.

What is the relevant cost of labour for the contract?

A $200

B $1,200

C $1,400

D $1,800

**(2 marks)**

**144 A company is evaluating a project that requires two types of material (T and V).**

Data relating to the material requirements are as follows:

| *Material type* | *Quantity needed for project* | *Quantity currently in inventory* | *Original cost of quantity in inventory* | *Current purchase price* | *Current resale price* |
|---|---|---|---|---|---|
| | kg | kg | $/kg | $/kg | $/kg |
| T | 500 | 100 | 40 | 45 | 44 |
| V | 400 | 200 | 55 | 52 | 40 |

Material T is regularly used by the company in normal production. Material V is no longer in use by the company and has no alternative use within the business.

What is the total relevant cost of materials for the project?

A $40,400

B $40,900

C $43,400

D $43,900

**(2 marks)**

**145 A company is evaluating a project that requires 4,000 kg of a material that is used regularly in normal production. 2,500 kg of the material, purchased last month at a total cost of $20,000, are in inventory. Since last month the price of the material has increased by 2.5 per cent.**

What is the total relevant cost of the material for the project?

A $12,300

B $20,500

C $32,300

D $32,800

**(2 marks)**

**146 A contract is under consideration that requires 800 labour hours to complete. There are 450 hours of spare labour capacity for which the workers are still being paid the normal rate of pay. The remaining hours required for the contract can be found either by overtime working paid at 50% above the normal rate of pay or by diverting labour from the manufacture of product OT. If the contract is undertaken and labour is diverted, then sales of product OT will be lost. Product OT takes seven labour hours per unit to manufacture and makes a contribution of $14 per unit. The normal rate of pay for labour is $8 per hour.**

What is the total relevant labour cost to the contract?

A $3,500

B $4,200

C $4,500

D $4,900

**(2 marks)**

**147 All of a company's skilled labour, which is paid $8 per hour, is fully employed manufacturing a product to which the following data refer:**

| | *$ per unit* | *$ per unit* |
|---|---|---|
| Selling price | | 60 |
| Less variable costs: | | |
| Skilled labour | 20 | |
| Others | 15 | |
| | | (35) |
| Contribution | | 25 |

The company is evaluating a contract that requires 90 skilled labour hours to complete. No other supplies of skilled labour are available.

What is the total relevant skilled labour cost of the contract?

A $720

B $900

C $1,620

D $2,160

**(2 marks)**

**148 A company requires 600 kg of raw material Z for a contract it is evaluating. It has 400 kg of material Z in inventory that was purchased last month. Since then the purchase price of material Z has risen by 8% to $27 per kg. Raw material Z is used regularly by the company in normal production.**

What is the total relevant cost of raw material Z to the contract?

A $15,336

B $15,400

C $16,200

D $17,496

**(2 marks)**

**149 Equipment owned by a company has a net book value of $1,800 and has been idle for some months. It could now be used on a six months contract that is being considered. If not used on this contract, the equipment would be sold now for a net amount of $2,000. After use on the contract, the equipment would have no saleable value and would be dismantled. The cost of dismantling and disposing of it would be $800.**

What is the total relevant cost of the equipment to the contract?

A $1,200

B $1,800

C $2,000

D $2,800

**(2 marks)**

## DEALING WITH LIMITING FACTORS

**The following information is to be used for questions 150, 151 and 152**

Buttercup manufactures and sells three products (R, S and T). These products are made using the same machinery. The total machining time available each month is 10,500 hours but this is insufficient to produce all the units of R, S and T required to meet maximum demands. No inventories of these products are held.

The following information is available:

| | *Product R* | *Product S* | *Product T* |
|---|---|---|---|
| Selling price per unit | $60 | $75 | $84 |
| Contribution to sales ratio | 20% | 24% | 25% |
| Machining minutes per unit | 40 | 54 | 75 |
| Maximum monthly demand (units) | 9,000 | 6,000 | 3,000 |

**150 The monthly shortfall in machining hours is:**

A 4,650 hours

B 3,600 hours

C 3,350 hours

D 3,250 hours

**(2 marks)**

**151 The monthly production plan in units that will maximise the company's total contribution from products R, S and T is:**

| | R | S | T |
|---|---|---|---|
| A | 9,000 | 830 | 3,000 |
| B | 9,000 | 5,000 | 0 |
| C | 7,650 | 6,000 | 0 |
| D | 2,024 | 6,000 | 3,000 |

**(2 marks)**

**152 The total contribution is:**

A 198,000

B 199,800

C 209,700

D 228,000

**(2 marks)**

---

**The following information relates to questions 153 and 154:**

A company that manufactures and sells two products (X and Y) aims to maximise its profits. It holds no inventory. Product X makes a contribution per unit of $4 and product Y makes a contribution per unit of $1.

Next period the company faces three 'less than' production constraints and these are shown as the lines labelled (1), (2) and (3) on the following graph:

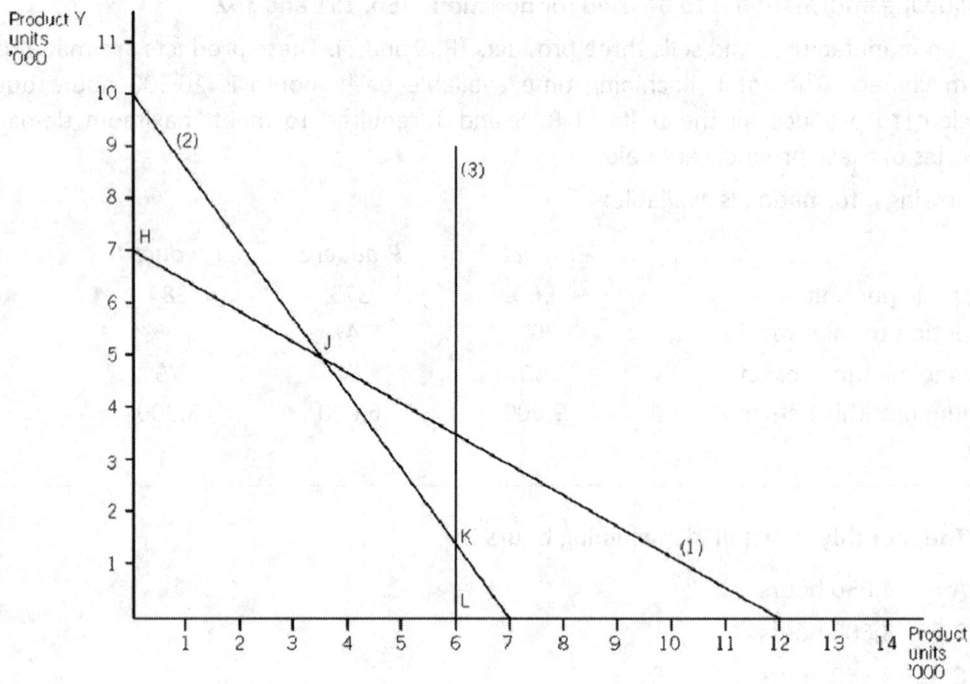


---

**153 Which of the following points shown on the graph is optimal for next period?**

A Point H

B Point J

C Point K

D Point L

**(2 marks)**

**154 Which of the following constraint formulations is represented by the line labelled (2) on the graph?**

| | | | | | |
|---|---|---|---|---|---|
| A | 10X | + | 7Y | ≤ | 70,000 |
| B | 7X | + | 10Y | ≤ | 70,000 |
| C | 7X | + | 13Y | ≤ | 91,000 |
| D | 13X | + | 7Y | ≤ | 91,000 |

**(2 marks)**

**155 A company manufactures two products (L and M) using the same material and labour. It holds no inventory. Information about the variable costs and maximum demands are as follows:**

| | *Product L* | *Product M* |
|---|---|---|
| | *$/unit* | *$/unit* |
| Material ($4 per litre) | 13 | 19 |
| Labour ($7 per hour) | 35 | 28 |
| | *Units* | *Units* |
| Maximum monthly demand | 6,000 | 8,000 |

Each month 50,000 litres of material and 60,000 labour hours are available.

Which one of the following statements is correct?

A Material is a limiting factor but labour is not a limiting factor.

B Material is not a limiting factor but labour is a limiting factor.

C Neither material nor labour is a limiting factor.

D Both material and labour are limiting factors.

**(2 marks)**

**156 A company manufactures and sells two products (L and M) both of which utilise the same material. For the coming period, the supply of material is limited to 5,000 kg. Data relating to each product are as follows:**

| *Product* | *X* | *Y* |
|---|---|---|
| Selling price per unit | $25 | $46 |
| Variable cost per unit | $15 | $10 |
| Material per unit (kgs) | 2.5 | 6 |
| Maximum demand (units) per period | 1,500 | 600 |

In order to maximise profit in the coming period, how many units of each product should the company manufacture and sell?

A 1,500 units of X and 208 units of Y

B 1,000 units of X and 417 units of Y

C 1,500 units of X and 600 units of Y

D 560 units of X and 600 units of Y

**(2 marks)**

**157 A company uses limiting factor analysis to calculate an optimal production plan given a scarce resource.**

The following applies to the three products of the company:

| Product | *I* | *II* | *III* |
|---|---|---|---|
| | $ | $ | $ |
| Direct materials (at $6/kg) | 36 | 24 | 15 |
| Direct labour (at $10/hour) | 40 | 25 | 10 |
| Variable overheads ($2/hour) | 8 | 5 | 2 |
| | 84 | 54 | 27 |
| Maximum demand (units) | 2,000 | 4,000 | 4,000 |
| Optimal production plan | 2,000 | 1,500 | 4,000 |

How many kg of material were available for use in production?

A 15,750 kg

B 28,000 kg

C 30,000 kg

D 38,000 kg

**(2 marks)**

**158 Which of the following is correct?**

A When considering limiting factors the products should always be ranked according to contribution per unit sold.

B If there is only one scarce resource linear programming should be used.

C In linear programming the point furthest from the origin will always be the point of profit maximisation.

D The slope of the objective function depends on the contributions of the products.

**(2 marks)**

**159 GR is currently experiencing a shortage of skilled labour. In the coming quarter only 3,600 hours will be available for the production of the firm's three products for which details are shown below:**

| *Product* | *X* | *Y* | *Z* |
|---|---|---|---|
| Selling price per unit | $66 | $100 | $120 |
| Variable cost per unit | $42 | $75 | $90 |
| Fixed cost per unit | $30 | $34 | $40 |
| Skilled labour per unit | 0.40 hours | 0.50 hours | 0.75 hours |
| Maximum quarterly demand | 5,000 | 5,000 | 2,000 |

The optimum production plan that will maximise profit for the quarter is:

| | Xs | Ys | Zs |
|---|---|---|---|
| A | 0 | 2,200 | 2,000 |
| B | 5,000 | 200 | 2,000 |
| C | 5,000 | 3,200 | 0 |
| D | 9,000 | 0 | 0 |

**(2 marks)**

**160 A company makes three products as follows:**

| | *Kilts* | *Skirts* | *Dresses* |
|---|---|---|---|
| | $ | $ | $ |
| Material at $5 per square metre | 5.0 | 2.50 | 10.0 |
| Labour At $2 Per Hour | 6.0 | 2.00 | 2.0 |
| Fixed costs absorbed | 6.0 | 2.00 | 2.0 |
| Profit | 6.0 | 3.50 | 5.0 |
| Sales price | 23.0 | 10.00 | 19.0 |

Maximum demand is 1,000 for each product, but supplies of material are limited to 4,000 square metres while the labour force will only work 1,000 hours.

To maximise its profits the company should produce:

A 1,000 kilts

B 1,000 skirts

C 1,000 dresses

D 333 kilts

**(2 marks)**

**The following information should be used for questions 161, 162 and 163**

A company manufactures and sells two products (X and Y) that have contributions per unit of $30 and $12 respectively. The company aims to maximise profit. Two materials (G and H) are used in the manufacture of each product. Each material is in short supply – 2,000 kg of G and 2,700 kg of H are available next period. The company holds no inventory and it can sell all the units produced.

The management accountant has drawn the following graph showing the constraints for materials G and H.

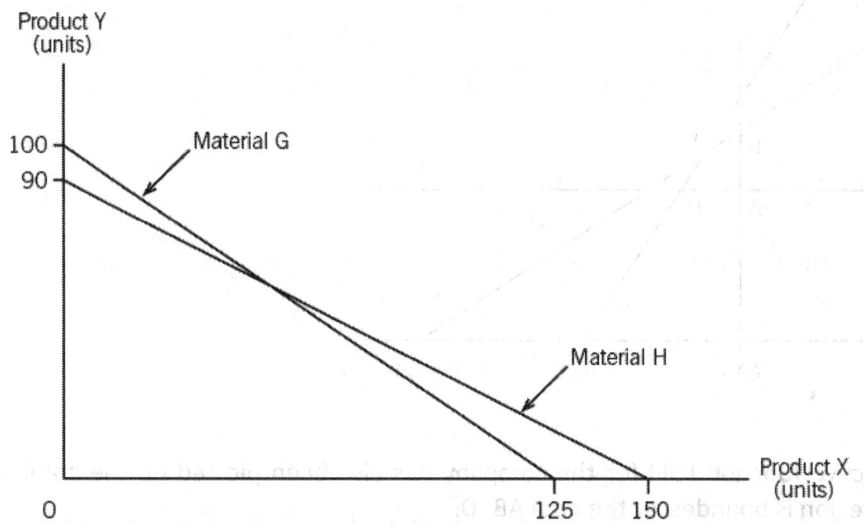

**161 What is the amount (in kg) of material G and material H used in each unit of product Y?**

| | *Material G* | *Material H* |
|---|---|---|
| A | 20 | 30 |
| B | 20 | 20 |
| C | 30 | 30 |
| D | 30 | 20 |

**(2 marks)**

**162 What is the intersection of the constraints for material G and material H?**

A X = 50, Y = 30

B X = 60, Y = 30

C X = 60, Y = 50

D X = 50, Y = 60

**(2 marks)**

**163 What is the optimal mix of production (in units) for the next period?**

| | *Product X* | *Product Y* |
|---|---|---|
| A | 0 | 90 |
| B | 50 | 60 |
| C | 60 | 50 |
| D | 125 | 0 |

**(2 marks)**

**164 The following graph has been established for a given set of constraints:**

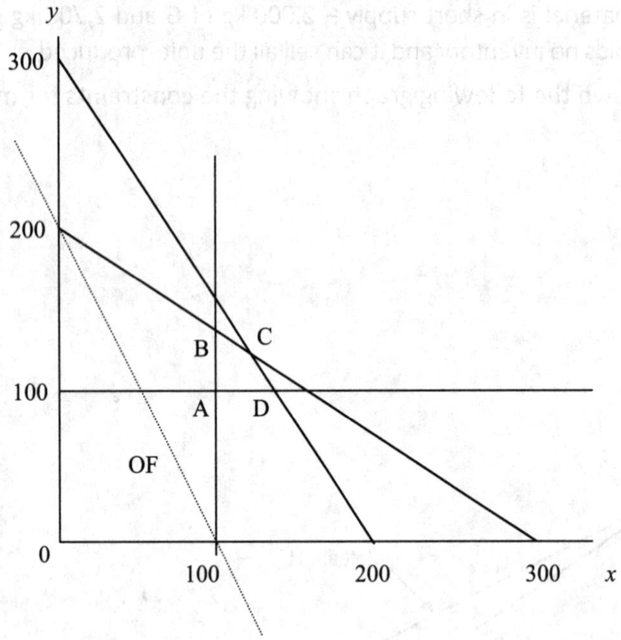


The objective function (OF) for the company has also been plotted on the graph and the feasible region is bounded by the area ABCD.

At which point on the graph will profits be maximised?

A Point A

B Point B

C Point C

D Point D

**(2 marks)**

**165 Taree uses linear programming to establish the optimal production plan for its two products, A and U, given that it has the objective of minimising costs.**

The following graph has been established bearing in mind the various constraints of the business. The clear area indicates the feasible region.

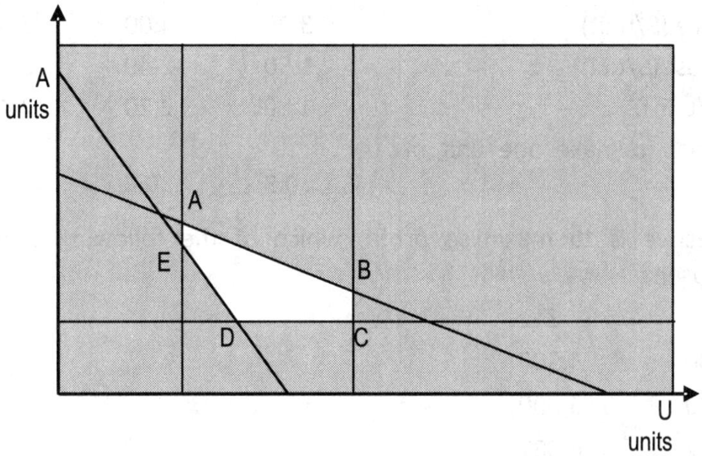


Which points are most likely to give the optimal solution?

A A or B only

B A, B or C only

C D or E only

D B, D or E only

**(2 marks)**

**166 The following graph relates to a linear programming problem:**

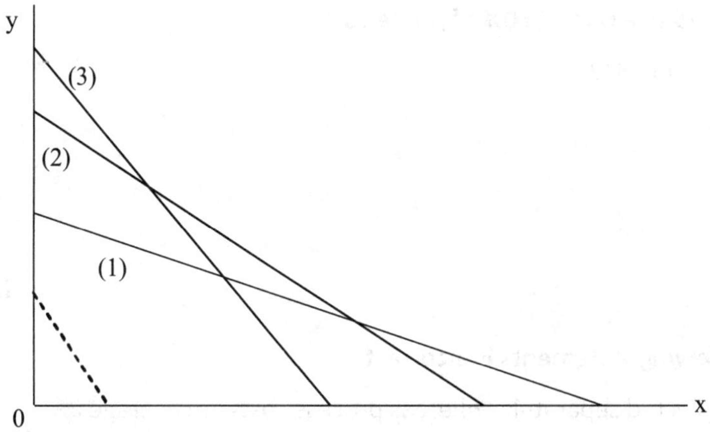


The objective is to maximise total contribution and the dotted line on the graph depicts this function. There are three constraints which are all of the 'less than or equal' type which are depicted on the graph as the three solid lines labelled (1), (2) and (3).

Constraint 1 is represented by the line 12.5X + 25Y = 1,375

Constraint 2 is represented by the line 17.5X + 20Y = 1,325

What is the intersection of constraints 1 and 2?

A X = 40, Y = 30

B X = 30, Y = 40

C X = 35, Y = 40

D X = 40, Y = 35

**(2 marks)**

**167 A company has only 6,000 kg of an irreplaceable raw material that can be used to make three possible products X, Y and Z, details of which are given below:**

| | *X* | *Y* | *Z* |
|---|---|---|---|
| Maximum demand (units) | 4,000 | 3,000 | 5,000 |
| Constant unit selling price ($/unit) | 3.00 | 4.00 | 5.00 |
| Constant unit variable cost ($/unit) | 1.50 | 2.40 | 2.60 |
| Allocated fixed costs ($/unit) | 1.80 | 2.20 | 2.40 |
| Quantity of raw material to make one unit of product (kg) | 0.3 | 0.4 | 0.8 |

If the company's objective is to maximise profit, which of the following production schedules should be chosen?

| | *X* | *Y* | *Z* |
|---|---|---|---|
| A | 4,000 | 3,000 | 4,500 |
| B | 4,000 | 2,000 | 5,000 |
| C | 3,750 | 2,812 | 4,687 |
| D | 2,666 | 3,000 | 5,000 |

**(2 marks)**

# JOB, BATCH AND PROCESS COSTING

**168 A company operates a job costing system. Job 812 requires $60 of direct materials, $40 of direct labour and $20 of direct expenses. Direct labour is paid $8 per hour. Production overheads are absorbed at a rate of $16 per direct labour hour and non-production overheads are absorbed at a rate of 60% of prime cost.**

What is the total cost of Job 812?

A $240

B $260

C $272

D $320

**(2 marks)**

**169 Which one of the following statements is incorrect?**

A Job costs are collected separately, whereas process costs are averages.

B In job costing the progress of a job can be ascertained from the materials requisition notes and job tickets or time sheet.

C In process costing information is needed about work passing through a process and work remaining in each process.

D In process costing, but not job costing, the cost of normal loss will be incorporated into normal product costs.

**(2 marks)**

**The following data are to be used for questions 170 and 171**

A firm uses job costing and recovers overheads on a direct labour cost basis.

Three jobs were worked on during a period, the details of which were:

| | *Job 1* | *Job 2* | *Job 3* |
|---|---|---|---|
| | $ | $ | $ |
| Opening work-in-progress | 8,500 | 0 | 46,000 |
| Material in period | 17,150 | 29,025 | 0 |
| Labour for period | 12,500 | 23,000 | 4,500 |

The overheads for the period were exactly as budgeted, $140,000. Actual labour costs were also the same as budgeted.

Jobs 1 and 2 were the only incomplete jobs at the end of the period.

**170 What was the value of closing work-in-progress?**

A $81,900

B $90,175

C $140,675

D $214,425

**(2 marks)**

**171 Job 3 was completed during the period and consisted of 2,400 identical circuit boards. The firm adds 50% to total production costs to arrive at a selling price.**

What is the selling price of a circuit board?

A It cannot be calculated without more information

B $31.56

C $41.41

D $58.33

**(2 marks)**

**172 A company uses process costing to value output. During the last month the following information was recorded:**

| | |
|---|---|
| Output: | 2,800 kg valued at $7.50/kg |
| Normal loss: | 300 kg which has a scrap value of $3/kg |
| Actual gain: | 100 kg |

What was the value of the input?

A $22,650

B $21,900

C $21,600

D $21,150

**(2 marks)**

**173 ABC manufactures product X in a single process. Normal loss (scrap) in the process is 10% of output and scrapped units can be sold off for $4/unit.**

In period 8 there was no opening inventory and no closing inventory. Process costs of direct materials, direct labour and production overheads totalled $184,800. Input to the process in the month was 13,200 units.

What was the cost/unit produced?

A $12.50

B $15.00

C $15.15

D $15.40

**(2 marks)**

**174 A company uses process costing to value its output. The following was recorded for the period:**

| | |
|---|---|
| Input materials | 2,000 units at $4.50 per unit |
| Conversion costs | $13,340 |
| Normal loss | 5% of input valued at $3 per unit |
| Abnormal loss | 150 units |

There were no opening or closing inventories.

What was the valuation of one unit of output?

A $11.80

B $11.60

C $11.20

D $11.00

**(2 marks)**

**175 A company that operates a process costing system had work-in-progress at the start of last month of 300 units (valued at $1,710) that were 60% complete in respect of all costs.**

Last month a total of 2,000 units were completed and transferred to the finished goods warehouse. The cost per equivalent unit for costs arising last month was $10. The company uses the FIFO method of cost allocation.

What was the total value of the 2,000 units transferred to the finished goods warehouse last month?

A $19,910

B $20,000

C $20,510

D $21,710

**(2 marks)**

**176 Vare produces various inks at its Normanton factory. Production details for Process 1 are as follows:**

| | | |
|---|---|---|
| Opening work-in-progress, 1 April | 400 units | 60% complete |
| Closing work-in-progress, 30 April | 600 units | 20% complete |
| Units started | 1,000 | |
| Units finished | 800 | |

The degree of completion quoted relates to labour and overhead costs. Three-quarters of the materials are added at the start of the process and the remaining quarter added when the process is 50% complete. The company uses the FIFO method of cost allocation.

The equivalent units of production for materials in the period are:

A 1,250

B 1,000

C 850

D 680

**(2 marks)**

**177 Two products W and X are created from a joint process. Both products can be sold immediately after split-off. There are no opening inventories or wok-in-progress. The following information is available for the last period :**

Total joint production costs $776,160

| **Product** | **Production units** | **Sales units** | **Selling Price per unit** |
|---|---|---|---|
| W | 12,000 | 10,000 | $10 |
| X | 10,000 | 8,000 | $12 |

Using the sales value method of apportioning joint production costs, what was the value of the closing inventory of product X for the last period?

A $68,992

B $70,560

C $76,032

D $77,616

**(2 marks)**

**178 In a process where there are no work-in-progress inventories, two joint products (J and K) are created. Information (in units) relating to last month is as follows:**

| *Product* | *Sales* | *Opening inventory of finished goods* | *Closing inventory of finished goods* |
|---|---|---|---|
| J | 6,000 | 100 | 300 |
| K | 4,000 | 400 | 200 |

Joint production costs last month were $110,000 and these were apportioned to joint products based on the number of units produced.

What were the joint production costs apportioned to product J for last month?

A $63,800

B $64,000

C $66,000

D $68,200

**(2 marks)**

**179 Charleville operates a continuous process producing three products and one by-product. Output from the process for a month was as follows:**

| *Product* | *Selling price per unit* | *Units of output from process* |
|---|---|---|
| 1 | $18 | 10,000 |
| 2 | $25 | 20,000 |
| 3 | $20 | 20,000 |
| 4 (by-product) | $2 | 3,500 |

Total joint costs were $277,000.

What was the unit cost valuation for product 3 using the sales revenue basis for allocating joint costs assuming that the revenue receivable from the by-product is deducted from the joint costs?

A $4.70

B $4.80

C $5.00

D $5.10

**(2 marks)**

**180 A business operates a job costing system and prices its jobs by adding 20% to the total cost of the job. The prime cost of a job was $6,840 and it had used 156 direct labour hours. The fixed production overheads are absorbed on the basis of direct labour hours. The budgeted overhead absorption rate was based upon a budgeted fixed overhead of $300,000 and total budgeted direct labour hours of 60,000.**

The job should be sold for:

A $7,620

B $8,208

C $9,144

D $9,525

**(2 marks)**

**181 In process costing, if an abnormal loss arises the process account is generally:**

A debited with the scrap value of the abnormal loss units

B debited with the full production cost of the abnormal loss units

C credited with the scrap value of the abnormal loss units

D credited with the full production cost of the abnormal loss units.

**(2 marks)**

**182 X uses process costing. In Process 3 the normal loss is 4% of total input.**

Last period the input from Process 2 was 8,500 kg and additional material of 4,250 kg was added to process 3.

Actual output to finished goods was 12,700 kg.

There was no opening or closing work-in-progress in the period.

The abnormal gain or loss in kg for period 3 was:

A 460 kg gain

B 460 kg loss

C 290 kg gain

D 290 kg loss

**(2 marks)**

**183 A chemical process has a normal wastage of 10% of input. In a period, 2,500 kg of material were input and there was an abnormal loss of 75 kg.**

The quantity of good production achieved was:

A 2,175 kg

B 2,250 kg

C 2,325 kg

D 2,675 kg

**(2 marks)**

**184 A company operates a job costing system.**

Job number 605 requires $300 of direct materials and $400 of direct labour. Direct labour is paid at the rate of $8 per hour. Production overheads are absorbed at a rate of $26 per direct labour hour and non-production overheads are absorbed at a rate of 120% of prime cost.

What is the total cost of job number 605?

A $2,000

B $2,400

C $2,840

D $4,400

**(2 marks)**

**185 A factory manufactures model cars. During October work commenced on 110,000 new cars. This was in addition to 20,000 that were 50% complete at the start of the month. At the end of October there were 40,000 cars that were 50% complete.**

Costs for October were:

| | $000 |
|---|---|
| Brought forward | 11,000 |
| Incurred this period | 121,000 |
| | $132,000 |

If this factory chooses the weighted average method of spreading costs, what is the cost per car for October production?

A $1,100

B $1,200

C $1,210

D $1,320

**(2 marks)**

**186 In a production process the percentage completion of the work-in-progress (WIP) at the end of a period is found to have been understated.**

When this is corrected what will be the effect on the cost per unit and the total value of the WIP?

| | *Cost per unit* | *Total value of WIP* |
|---|---|---|
| A | Decrease | Decrease |
| B | Decrease | Increase |
| C | Increase | Decrease |
| D | Increase | Increase |

**(2 marks)**

**187 The following information is available for a production process for the last period:**

| | |
|---|---|
| Material input | 200 kg at $4 per kg |
| Labour input | 100 hours at $15 per hour |
| Department overhead | $1,000 |
| Transfer to finished goods | 150 kg |

Normal loss is 10% of input. Losses are identified when the process is 50% complete.

There is no opening or closing work-in-progress.

The total cost of a completed unit is:

A $22.00

B $20.48

C $19.59

D $18.33

**(2 marks)**

**188 At the start of the month, there were 2,000 units of work-in-progress in a factory. During the month, 12,000 units were started. At the end of the month, 3,000 units were in closing work in progress. The degree of completion of opening work-in-progress was 70% and closing work in progress was 20%.**

How many equivalent units of production were achieved during the month?

A 10,200

B 11,000

C 11,600

D 14,000

**(2 marks)**

**189 The following information is available for a production process for the last period:**

| | |
|---|---|
| Material input | 200 kg at $6 per kg |
| Labour and overhead input | $3,500 |
| Transfer to finished goods | 190 kg |

Normal loss is 15% of input and has a scrap value of $1 per kg.

There is no opening or closing work-in-progress.

The value of the finished output for the period (to the nearest $) is:

A $4,465

B $4,670

C $5,219

D $5,253 **(2 marks)**

**190 Which of the following are features of process costing?**

(i) Homogeneous products

(ii) Customer-driven production

(iii) Finished goods are valued at an average cost per unit

A (i) and (iii)

B (ii) and (iii)

C (iii) only

D (i) only **(2 marks)**

**191 A builder has produced a quote for some alterations. The price is made up as follows:**

| | | $ |
|---|---|---|
| Direct materials | 100 kg @ $4 per kg | 400 |
| Direct labour | 5 hours @ $10 per hour | 50 |
| | 15 hours @ $5 per hour | 75 |
| Hire of machine | 1 day @ $100 per day | 100 |
| Overheads | 20 hours @ $8 per hour | 160 |
| Total cost | | 785 |
| Profit mark-up @ 20% | 0.2 × $785 | 157 |
| Price quoted | | $942 |

Actual costs for the job were as follows:

| | |
|---|---|
| Direct materials | 120 kg @ $4 per kg |
| Direct labour | 3 hours @ $10 per hour |
| | 20 hours @ $5 per hour |
| Hire of machine | 2 days @ $100 per day |

The actual profit/(loss) made on the job was:

A $52 loss

B $28 loss

C $28 profit

D $52 profit

**(2 marks)**

# SERVICE AND OPERATION COSTING

**192 Which of the following would be considered a service industry?**

(i) An airline company

(ii) A railway company

(iii) A firm of accountants

A (i) and (ii) only

B (ii) and (iii) only

C (i), (ii) and (iii)

**(1 mark)**

**193 Which of the following are characteristics of service costing?**

(i) High levels of indirect costs as a proportion of total cost.

(ii) Use of equivalent units.

(iii) Use of composite cost units.

(iv) Long timescale from commencement to completion of the cost unit.

A (i) and (iv) only

B (iii) only

C (i) and (iii) only

D All of them

**(2 marks)**

**194 Which of the following is NOT likely to be used in a hospital run by a charitable foundation?**

A Cost per patient

B Cost per bed-day

C Bed throughput

D Profit per patient

**(2 marks)**

**195 A hotel calculates a number of statistics including average cost per occupied bed per day.**

The following information is provided for a 30-day period.

| | *Rooms with twin beds* | *Single rooms* |
|---|---|---|
| Number of rooms in hotel | 260 | 70 |
| Number of rooms available to let | 240 | 40 |
| Average number of rooms occupied daily | 200 | 30 |

| | |
|---|---|
| Number of guests in period | 6,450 |
| Average length of stay | 2 days |
| Payroll costs for period | $100,000 |
| Cost of cleaning supplies in period | $5,000 |
| Total cost of laundering in period | $22,500 |

The average cost per occupied bed per day for the period is:

A $9.90

B $9.88

C $7.20

D $8.17

**(2 marks)**

**The following information should be used for questions 196 and 197**

A hospital has forecast the following information regarding a general surgical procedure for the year ending 31 December 20X6:

| | |
|---|---|
| Number of treatments | 950 |
| Average length of stay per treatment | 2 days |
| Nursing time per patient per day | 2 hours |
| Standard fee | $7,000 |
| Drugs cost per treatment | $780 |
| Accommodation costs | $200 per day |
| Nursing time | $50 per hour |
| Doctors' salaries | $3,600,000 |
| General overheads | $1,500,000 |

**196 What is the contribution per treatment?**

A $5,620

B $5,720

C $5,820

D $5,920

**(2 marks)**

**197 What is the margin of safety?**

A 43 treatments

B 126 treatments

C 132 treatments

D 907 treatments

**(2 marks)**

**198 The following figures relate to two electricity supply companies.**

**Meter reading, billing and collection costs**

| | *Company A* | *Company B* |
|---|---|---|
| Total cost ($000) | 600 | 1,000 |
| Units sold (millions) | 2,880 | 9,600 |
| Number of consumers (thousands) | 800 | 1,600 |
| Sales of electricity (millions) | $18 | $50 |

The figures given indicate that Company A is more efficient than Company B.

This statement is:

A True

B False

**(1 mark)**

**199 A hotel calculates a number of statistics including average room occupancy.**

Average room occupancy is calculated as the total number of rooms occupied as a percentage of rooms available to let.

The following information is provided for a 30-day period.

| | *Rooms with twin beds* | *Single rooms* |
|---|---|---|
| Number of rooms in hotel | 260 | 70 |
| Number of rooms available to let | 240 | 40 |
| Average number of rooms occupied daily | 200 | 30 |

The average room occupancy is:

A 69.7%

B 82.1%

C 82.7%

D 84.8%

**(2 marks)**

**200 Which of the following are features of service organisations?**

(i) High levels of inventory

(ii) High proportion of fixed costs

(iii) Difficulty in identifying suitable cost units

A (i) and (ii) only

B (i) and (iii) only

C (ii) and (iii) only

D All of these

**(2 marks)**

# BUDGETING

**201 The main purposes of budgeting are:**

(i) to give authority to spend

(ii) to control expenditure

(iii) to aid decision making.

A (i) only

B (i) and (ii) only

C (ii) only

D (i), (ii) and (iii)

**(2 marks)**

**202 The budget committee is made up of representatives from the finance function and co-ordinates the budget planning process.**

This statement is:

A True

B False

**(1 mark)**

**203 A company manufactures and sells a single product. The following data have been extracted from the current year's budget.**

| | |
|---|---|
| Sales and production (units) | 5,000 |
| Variable cost per unit | $50 |
| Fixed cost per unit | $70 |
| C/S (contribution/sales) ratio | 75% |

The selling price per unit for next year is budgeted to increase by 8%, whereas both the variable cost per unit and the total fixed costs are expected to increase by 12%.

Calculate the number of units that should be produced and sold next year in order to achieve the same profit as in the current year.

A 4,688

B 4,950

C 5,209

D 5,280

**(2 marks)**

**204 A business is preparing its production budget for the year ahead for product A998. It is estimated that 100,000 units of A998 can be sold in the year and the opening inventory is currently 14,000 units. The inventory level is to be reduced by 40% by the end of the year.**

The number of units of A998 needed to be produced is:

A 86,000

B 94,400

C 100,000

D 108,400

**(2 marks)**

**205 The production budget is calculated by taking the sales budget adding the opening inventory of finished goods and subtracting the closing inventory of finished goods.**

This statement is:

A True

B False

**(1 mark)**

**206 A process has a normal loss of 10% and budgeted output is 4,500 litres for the period. Opening inventory of raw material is 600 litres and is expected to increase by 20% by the end of the period.**

The material usage budget is:

A 4,500 litres

B 5,000 litres

C 5,133 litres

D 5,120 litres

**(2 marks)**

**207 The material usage budget is calculated by taking the production budget and multiplying by the standard material quantity per unit.**

This statement is:

A True

B False

**(1 mark)**

**208 A company has a budget for two products A and B as follows:**

| | *Product A* | *Product B* |
|---|---|---|
| Sales (units) | 2,000 | 4,500 |
| Production (units) | 1,750 | 5,000 |
| Labour: | | |
| Skilled at $10/hour | 2 hours/unit | 2 hours/unit |
| Unskilled at $7/hour | 3 hours/unit | 4 hours/unit |

What is the budgeted cost for unskilled labour for the period?

A $105,000

B $135,000

C $176,750

D $252,500

**(2 marks)**

**209 The volume variance is the difference between the flexible budget and the actual results.**

This statement is:

A True

B False

**(1 mark)**

**The following information should be used for questions 210 and 211**

Oswald Press produces and sells textbooks for schools and colleges. The following budgeted information is available for the year ending 31 December 20X6:

| | *Budget* | *Actual* |
|---|---|---|
| Sales (units) | 120,000 | 100,000 |
| | $000 | $000 |
| Sales revenue | 1,200 | 995 |
| Variable printing costs | 360 | 280 |
| Variable production overheads | 60 | 56 |
| Fixed production cost | 300 | 290 |
| Fixed administration cost | 360 | 364 |
| Profit | 120 | 5 |

**210 The flexed budget shows:**

A a profit of $10,000

B a loss of $10,000

C a profit of $100,000

D a loss of $100,000

**(2 marks)**

**211 The total expenditure and volume variances are:**

| | Expenditure variance | Volume variance |
|---|---|---|
| A | $15,000 favourable | $130,000 adverse |
| B | $95,000 adverse | $115,000 favourable |
| C | $115,000 adverse | $95,000 favourable |
| D | $130,000 adverse | $15,000 favourable |

**(2 marks)**

**212 The principal budget factor for a footwear retailer is:**

A The cost item taking the largest share of total expenditure.

B The product line contributing the largest amount to sales revenue.

C The product line contributing the largest amount to business profits.

D The constraint that is expected to limit the retailer's activities during the budget period.

**(2 marks)**

**213 A company makes 2 products, X and Y, which are sold in the ratio 1:2. The selling prices are $50 and $100 respectively. The company wants to earn $100,000 over the next period. The sales budget should be:**

| | X (units) | Y (units) |
|---|---|---|
| A | 1,334 | 667 |
| B | 800 | 400 |
| C | 667 | 1,334 |
| D | 400 | 800 |

*(2 marks)*

**214 A budget manual will include which of the following?**

(i) An organisation chart

(ii) A budget timetable

(iii) Copies of budget forms

(iv) Key assumptions to be used in the budget

A (ii), (iii) and (iv)

B (ii) and (iv)

C (iii) and (iv)

D all of these

**(2 marks)**

**215 A business is preparing its production budget, materials usage and materials purchases budget for the forthcoming period. The following information is known:**

| | |
|---|---|
| Budgeted sales | 2,300 units |
| Current inventory of finished goods | 400 units |
| Required closing inventory of finished goods | 550 units |

Each unit of the product uses 6 kg of material X and details of this are as follows:

| | |
|---|---|
| Current inventory of X | 2,000 kg |
| Required closing inventory of X | 2,600 kg |

The amount of production volume required for the forthcoming period to meet the sales demand is:

A 3,050 units

B 2,450 units

C 2,300 units

D 2,150 units

**(2 marks)**

**216 A company makes three products, X, Y and Z. The following information is available:**

| | X | Y | Z |
|---|---|---|---|
| Budgeted production (units) | 200 | 400 | 300 |
| Machine hours per unit | 5 | 6 | 2 |

| | |
|---|---|
| Variable overheads | $2.30 per machine hour |
| Fixed overheads | $0.75 per machine hour |

The overhead budget is:

A $12,200

B $12,000

C $11,590

D $10,980

**(2 marks)**

**The following information should be used for questions 217, 218 and 219**

A toy manufacturer produces two products, a clockwork clown and a wind-up train. Standard cost data for the products are as follows:

| | *Clockwork clown* | *Wind-up train* |
|---|---|---|
| Direct materials ($5 per kg) | 2 kg | 1 kg |
| Direct labour ($8 per hour) | 18 minutes | 30 minutes |
| Budgeted sales | 450 | 550 |
| Budgeted inventories are as follows: | | |
| Finished goods | | |
| Opening inventory | 20 | 50 |
| Closing inventory | 30 | 40 |
| Raw materials | | |
| Opening inventory | 50 kg | |
| Closing inventory | 60 kg | |

**217 The total direct material usage budget is:**

A 1,540 kg

B 1,470 kg

C 1,460 kg

D 1,440 kg

**(2 marks)**

**218 The total direct material purchases budget is:**

A $7,350

B $7,300

C $7,250

D $7,200

**(2 marks)**

**219 The total direct labour budget is:**

A $3,264

B $3,280

C $3,290

D $3,296

**(2 marks)**

**220 A job requires 2,400 actual labour hours for completion but it is anticipated that idle time will be 20% of the total time required. If the wage rate is $10 per hour, what is the budgeted labour cost for the job, including the cost of the idle time?**

A $19,200

B $24,000

C $28,800

D $30,000

**(2 marks)**

# STANDARD COSTING

**221 Which of the following techniques would be useful for controlling costs?**

(i) Actual versus flexed budget

(ii) Variance analysis

(iii) Trend of costs analysis

A (i) and (ii) only

B (i) and (iii) only

C (ii) and (iii) only

D (i), (ii) and (iii)

**(2 marks)**

**222 When considering setting standards for costing which of the following would NOT be appropriate?**

A The normal level of activity should always be used for absorbing overheads.

B Average prices for materials should be used, encompassing any discounts that are regularly available.

C The labour rate used will be the rate at which labour is paid.

D Average material usage should be established based on generally-accepted working practices.

**(2 marks)**

**223 A company uses standard marginal costing. Last month the standard contribution on actual sales was $10,000 and the following variances arose :**

| | |
|---|---|
| Total variable costs variance | $2,000 adverse |
| Sales Price variance | $500 favourable |
| Sales volume contribution variance | $1,000 adverse |

**What was the actual contribution for last month?**

A $7,000

B $7,500

C $8,000

D $8,500

**(2 marks)**

**224 A company uses standard marginal costing. Last month, when all sales were at the standard selling price, the standard contribution from actual sales was $50,000 and the following variances arose :**

| | |
|---|---|
| Total variable cost variance | $3,500 Adverse |
| Total fixed costs variance | $1,000 favourable |
| Sales volume contribution variance | $2,000 favourable |

**What was the actual contribution for last month?**

A $46,500

B $47,500

C $48,500

D $49,500

**(2 marks)**

**225 The following information relates to labour costs for the past month:**

| | | |
|---|---|---|
| Budget | Labour rate | $10 per hour |
| | Production time | 15,000 hours |
| | Time per unit | 3 hours |
| | Production units | 5,000 units |
| Actual | Wages paid | $176,000 |
| | Production | 5,500 units |
| | Total hours worked | 14,000 hours |

There was no idle time.

What were the labour rate and efficiency variances?

| | *Rate variance* | *Efficiency variance* |
|---|---|---|
| A | $26,000 adverse | $25,000 favourable |
| B | $26,000 adverse | $10,000 favourable |
| C | $36,000 adverse | $2,500 favourable |
| D | $36,000 adverse | $25,000 favourable |

**(2 marks)**

**226 The following details relate to product T, which has a selling price of $44.00:**

| | *$/unit* |
|---|---|
| Direct materials | 15.00 |
| Direct labour (3 hours) | 12.00 |
| Variable overhead | 6.00 |
| Fixed overhead | 4.00 |
| | 37.00 |

During April 20X6, the actual production of T was 800 units, which was 100 units fewer than budgeted. The budget shows an annual production target of 10,800, with fixed costs accruing at a constant rate throughout the year. Actual overhead expenditure totalled $8,500 for April 20X6.

Overheads are absorbed on the basis of units produced.

The overhead variances for April 20X6 were:

| | *Expenditure* | *Volume* |
|---|---|---|
| | $ | $ |
| A | 367 A | 1,000 A |
| B | 500 A | 400 A |
| C | 100 A | 1,000 A |
| D | 100 A | 400 A |

**(2 marks)**

**227 A company operates a standard marginal costing system. Last month its actual fixed overhead expenditure was 10% above budget resulting in a fixed overhead expenditure variance of $36,000.**

What was the actual expenditure on fixed overheads last month?

A $324,000

B $360,000

C $396,000

D $400,000

**(2 marks)**

**228 FGH has the following budgeted and actual data:**

| | |
|---|---:|
| Budgeted fixed overhead cost | $120,000 |
| Budgeted production (units) | 20,000 |
| Actual fixed overhead cost | $115,000 |
| Actual production (units) | 21,000 |

The fixed overhead volume variance:

A is $4,500 adverse

B is $5,500 favourable

C is $6,000 favourable

D is $10,500 favourable

**(2 marks)**

**229 A company budgeted to make 30,000 units of a product P. Each unit was expected to take 4 hours to make and budgeted fixed overhead expenditure was $840,000. Actual production of product P in the period was 32,000 units, which took 123,000 hours to make. Actual fixed overhead expenditure was $885,600.**

What was the fixed overhead capacity variance for the period?

A $21,000 favourable

B $21,000 adverse

C $35,000 adverse

D $56,000 favourable

**(2 marks)**

**230 QRL uses a standard absorption costing system. The following details have been extracted from its budget for April 20X7:**

| | |
|---|---:|
| Fixed production overhead cost | $48,000 |
| Production (units) | 4,800 |

In April 20X7 the fixed production overhead cost was under-absorbed by $8,000 and the fixed production overhead expenditure variance was $2,000 adverse.

The actual number of units produced was:

A 3,800

B 4,000

C 4,200

D 5,400

**(2 marks)**

**231 Performance standards that have remained unchanged over a long period of time are known as:**

A ideal standards

B current standards

C basic standards

D long-term standards.

**(2 marks)**

**232 Standard costing may be inappropriate in the modern business environment because quality is now as important, if not more, than price.**

This statement is:

A True

B False

**(1 mark)**

**233 A company has a higher than expected staff turnover and as a result staff are less experienced than expected.**

As an indirect result of this, are the labour rate variance and material usage variance likely to be adverse or favourable?

| | *Labour rate* | *Material usage* |
|---|---|---|
| A | Favourable | Favourable |
| B | Adverse | Favourable |
| C | Favourable | Adverse |
| D | Adverse | Adverse |

**(2 marks)**

**234 A company is obliged to buy sub-standard materials at lower than standard price because nothing else is available.**

As an indirect result of this purchase, are the materials usage variance and labour efficiency variance likely to be adverse or favourable?

| | *Materials usage* | *Labour efficiency* |
|---|---|---|
| A | Favourable | Favourable |
| B | Adverse | Favourable |
| C | Favourable | Adverse |
| D | Adverse | Adverse |

**(2 marks)**

**235 Fawley's direct labour cost data relating to last month were as follows:**

| | |
|---|---|
| Standard labour cost of actual hours worked | $116,000 |
| Standard hours worked | 30,000 |
| Standard rate per hour | $4 |
| Labour rate variance | $5,800 favourable |
| Labour efficiency variance | $4,000 favourable |

The actual rate of pay per hour was:

A $3.80

B $3.81

C $3.94

D $3.99

**(2 marks)**

**236 Michel has the following results.**

10,080 hours actually worked and paid costing $8,770

If the rate variance is $706 adverse, the efficiency variance $256 favourable, and 5,000 units were produced, what is the standard production time per unit?

A 1.95 hours

B 1.96 hours

C 2.07 hours

D 2.08 hours

**(2 marks)**

**237 An extract from the standard cost card for product CJ is as follows:**

| | |
|---|---|
| Direct labour (0.5 hours × $12) | $6 |

710 units of CJ were produced in the period and staff worked 378 hours at a total cost of $4,725. Of these hours 20 were lost due to a material shortage.

The labour efficiency variance is:

A $516 favourable

B $36 favourable

C $36 adverse

D $516 adverse

**(2 marks)**

**238 A company makes a single product. The following details are from the cost card for the product:**

| | |
|---|---|
| Direct labour | 10 hours at $5 per hour |
| Variable overhead | 10 hours at $1.50 per hour |

The actual results for the last period are:

500 units produced

| | |
|---|---|
| Labour | 4,800 hours |
| Variable overheads | $7,700 |

The variable overhead expenditure and efficiency variances are:

| | *Expenditure* | *Efficiency* |
|---|---|---|
| A | $300 A | $500 F |
| B | $300 F | $500 A |
| C | $500 A | $300 F |
| D | $500 F | $300 A |

**(2 marks)**

**239 A company uses standard absorption costing. The following data relate to last month:**

| | *Budget* | *Actual* |
|---|---|---|
| Sales and production (units) | 1,000 | 900 |
| | *Standard* | *Actual* |
| | $ | $ |
| Selling price per unit | 50 | 52 |
| Total production cost per unit | 39 | 40 |

What was the adverse sales volume profit variance last month?

A $1,000

B $1,100

C $1,200

D $1,300

**(2 marks)**

**240 A company operates a standard marginal costing system. Last month actual fixed overhead expenditure was 2% below budget and the fixed overhead expenditure variance was $1,250.**

What was the actual fixed overhead expenditure for last month?

A $61,250

B $62,475

C $62,500

D $63,750

**(2 marks)**

**241 A favourable sales volume variance is calculated as the difference in sales volumes multiplied by :**

A Standard contribution per unit

B Standard cost per unit

C Standard profit per unit

D Standard selling price per unit

**(2 marks)**

**242 The sales volume variance will be the same whether marginal or absorption costing is used.**

This statement is:

A True

B False

**(1 mark)**

---

**The following information relates to questions 243 and 244**

The standard direct material cost for a product is $50 per unit (12.5 kg at $4 per kg). Last month the actual amount paid for 45,600 kg of material purchased and used was $173,280 and the direct material usage variance was $15,200 adverse.

---

**243 What was the direct material price variance last month?**

A $8,800 adverse

B $8,800 favourable

C $9,120 adverse

D $9,120 favourable

**(2 marks)**

**244 What was the actual production last month?**

A 3,344 units

B 3,520 units

C 3,952 units

D 4,160 units

**(2 marks)**

**245 A new machine is purchased which is more expensive, but requires less labour to operate per unit.**

The impact on the fixed overhead variances will be:

| | *Expenditure variance* | *Volume variance* |
|---|---|---|
| A | Adverse | Adverse |
| B | Adverse | Favourable |
| C | Favourable | Favourable |
| D | Favourable | Favourable |

**(2 marks)**

**246 QR has budgeted to produce 4,000 units in January. Actual production was 3,700 units with fixed production overheads of $10,300. The standard fixed overhead cost per unit was 1.5 hours at $2.40 per hour. 5,800 actual production hours were worked.**

**What was the fixed overhead volume variance?**

A $1,080 favourable

B $480 favourable

C $480 adverse

D $1,080 adverse

**(2 marks)**

**247 Which of the following could be the cause of an adverse sales volume variance for garden furniture.**

(i) The company offers discounts on sales prices in order to maintain business.

(ii) Poor weather leads to a reduction in sales.

(iii) A strike in the factory causes a shortage of finished goods.

A (i) and (ii) only

B (i) and (iii) only

C (ii) and (iii) only

D (i), (ii) and (iii)

**(2 marks)**

**248 The following information relates to April production of product CK:**

| | *Actual* | *Budget* |
|---|---|---|
| Units produced | 580 | 600 |
| Input of material (kg) | 1,566 | 1,500 |
| Cost of material purchased and input | $77,517 | $76,500 |

What is the materials usage variance?

A $2,349 favourable

B $3,366 adverse

C $5,742 adverse

D $5,916 adverse

**(2 marks)**

**249 For product DR, the material price variance for the month of August was $1,000 (Favourable) and the material usage variance was $300 (Adverse).**

The standard material usage per unit is 3 kg, and the standard material price is $2 per kg. 500 units were produced in the period. Opening inventories of raw materials were 100 kg and closing inventories 400 kg.

Material purchases in the period were:

A 1,050 kg

B 1,350 kg

C 1,650 kg

D 1,950 kg

**(2 marks)**

**250 The following information relates to a month's production of product CN:**

| | *Budget* | *Actual* |
|---|---|---|
| Units produced | 600 | 580 |
| Input of material P (kg) | 1,500 | 1,566 |
| Cost of material P purchased and input | $25,500 | $25,839 |

What is the price variance for material P?

A $783 favourable

B $339 adverse

C $1,189 adverse

D $1,972 adverse

**(2 marks)**

**251 A company uses a standard absorption costing system. Last month budgeted production was 8,000 units and the standard fixed production overhead cost was $15 per unit. Actual production last month was 8,500 units and the actual fixed production overhead cost was $17 per unit.**

What was the total adverse fixed production overhead variance for last month?

A $7,500

B $16,000

C $17,000

D $24,500 **(2 marks)**

**252 A company is reviewing actual performance to budget to see where there are differences. The following standard information is relevant:**

| | *$ per unit* |
|---|---|
| Selling price | 50 |
| | — |
| Direct materials | 4 |
| Direct labour | 16 |
| Fixed production overheads | 5 |
| Variable production overheads | 10 |
| Fixed selling costs | 1 |
| Variable selling cost | 1 |
| | — |
| Total costs | 37 |
| | — |
| Budgeted sales units | 3,000 |
| Actual sales units | 3,500 |

What was the favourable sales volume variance using marginal costing?

A $9,500

B $7,500

C $7,000

D $6,500 **(2 marks)**

**253 A company uses variance analysis to control costs and revenues.**

Information concerning sales is as follows:

| | |
|---|---|
| Budgeted selling price | $15 per unit |
| Budgeted sales units | 10,000 |
| Budgeted profit per unit | $5 |
| | |
| Actual sales revenue | $151,500 |
| Actual units sold | 9,800 |

What is the sales volume profit variance?

A $500 favourable

B $1,000 favourable

C $1,000 adverse

D $3,000 adverse

**(2 marks)**

**254 A company operates a standard absorption costing system. The standard fixed production overhead rate is $15 per hour.**

The following data relate to last month:

| | |
|---|---|
| Actual hours worked | 5,500 |
| Budgeted hours | 5,000 |
| Standard hours for actual production | 4,800 |

What was the fixed production overhead capacity variance?

A $7,500 adverse

B $7,500 favourable

C $10,500 adverse

D $10,500 favourable

**(2 marks)**

**255 Direct labour cost data relating to last month is as follows:**

| | |
|---|---|
| Actual hours worked | 28,000 |
| Total direct labour cost | $117,600 |
| Direct labour rate variance | $8,400 adverse |
| Direct labour efficiency variance | $3,900 favourable |

To the nearest thousand hours, what were the standard labour hours for actual production last month?

A 31,000 hrs

B 29,000 hrs

C 27,000 hrs

D 25,000 hrs

**(2 marks)**

# APPENDIX: SPREADSHEETS

**256 The following statements relate to spreadsheets:**

(i) A spreadsheet consists of records and files.

(ii) Most spreadsheets have a facility to allow data within them to be displayed graphically.

(iii) A spreadsheet could be used to prepare a budgeted income statement.

(iv) A spreadsheet is the most suitable software for storing large volumes of data.

Which of the above statements are correct?

A (i) and (ii) only

B (i), (iii) and (iv) only

C (ii) and (iii) only

D (iii) and (iv) only

**(2 marks)**

**257 John has produced the following spreadsheet to calculate the correlation coefficient between average daily fruit and vegetable intake (measured in normal portions) and success in exams (number of passes above C grade).**

| | A | B | C | D | E | F |
|---|---|---|---|---|---|---|
| 1 | **Correlation** | | | | | |
| 2 | | Vitamins | Exam | | | |
| 3 | | x | y | xy | $x^2$ | $y^2$ |
| 4 | | 0 | 6 | | | |
| 5 | | 1 | 5 | | | |
| 6 | | 2 | 4 | | | |
| 7 | | 3 | 4 | | | |
| 8 | | 4 | 6 | | | |
| 9 | | 5 | 7 | | | |
| 10 | | 6 | 7 | | | |
| 11 | **Totals** | | | | | |
| 12 | | | | | | |
| 13 | **Correlation coefficient** | | = | | | |
| 14 | | | | | | |
| 15 | | | | | | |

What should the formula in cell D13 be?

A (6*D11-B11*C11)/((6*E11-B11^2)*(6*F11-C11^2))^0.5

B (7*D11-B11*C11)/((7*E11-B11^2)*(7*F11-C11^2))

C (7*D11-B11*C11)/((7*E11-B11^2)*(7*F11-C11^2))^0.5

D (6*D11-B11*C11)/((6*E11-B11^2)*(6*F11-C11^2))

**(2 marks)**

**258 Which of the following are advantages of spreadsheet software over manual approaches?**

(i) Security

(ii) Speed

(iii) Accuracy

(iv) Legibility

A All of them

B (ii), (iii) and (iv)

C (ii) and (iv)

D (i) and (iv)

**(2 marks)**

**259 A company manufactures a single product. In a computer spreadsheet the cells F1 to F12 contain the budgeted monthly sales units for the 12 months of next year in sequence with January sales in cell F1 and finishing with December sales in F12. The company policy is for the closing inventory of finished goods each month to be 10% of the budgeted sales units for the following month..**

**Which of the following formulae will generate the budgeted production (in units) for March next year?**

A =[F3 +(0.1*F4)]

B =[F3 -(0.1*F4)]

C =[(1.1*F3) - (0.1*F4)]

D =[(0.9*F3) +(0.1*F4)]

**(2 marks)**

**260 Which of the following is not one of the main aspects of formatting cells?**

A Wrapping text

B Using graphics

C Setting number specification, e.g. working to 2 decimal places

D Changing the font, size or colour of text

**(2 marks)**

## Section 2

# ANSWERS TO PRACTICE QUESTIONS

## THE NATURE AND PURPOSE OF MANAGEMENT ACCOUNTING

**1 D**

**2 A**

Reginald is only responsible for costs

**3 A**

Cost accounting can be used for inventory valuation to meet the requirements of both internal reporting and external financial reporting.

**4 B**

Cost accounting is not part of financial accounting.

**5 A**

Qualitative data is normally non-numerical. Information comes from both internal and external sources. Operational information is usually short-term (current) in nature.

**6 C**

The manager of a profit centre needs to know about the profits of the centre, i.e. revenues and costs. (Revenues only are appropriate for a revenue centre; costs only for a cost centre; and revenues, costs and assets employed for an investment centre.)

**7 C**

Lowering a selling price, presumably to increase sales volume, is a short-term decision/plan. The measures in A, B and D are not planning decisions at all: they are all monitoring/control activities.

**8 B**

Strategic planning is carried out by senior managers and is concerned with long-term planning. Both quantitative and qualitative information is used.

**9 C**

(i) ROCE compares profit to capital employed and is not a suitable measure for a profit centre as the manager does not have responsibility for capital employed.

(ii) Cost centres are found in all organisations.

(iii) The manager of a revenue centre is only responsible for revenues, not costs.

**10 B**

The information should be sufficiently accurate given time and cost constraints. Managers should be made aware of the degree of accuracy of the information.

**11 A**

The mixing and pouring departments are cost centres. The paint is not poured into tins until after the colour adding department so a litre tin would not be a suitable cost unit.

# TYPES OF COST AND COST BEHAVIOUR

**12 D**

Options B and C would begin from 0 and are clearly incorrect. Option A would be similar to the graph given except it would be flat at the top due to the maximum annual charge.

**13 A**

Variable cost per unit = [(\$274,000 – \$250,000) ÷ (15,000 – 12,000)] = \$8

Total fixed cost above 11,000 units = [\$274,000 – (15,000 × \$8)] = \$154,000

Total fixed cost below 11,000 units = (10 ÷ 11) × \$154,000 = \$140,000

Total cost for 10,000 units = [(10,000 × \$8) + \$140,000] = \$220,000

**14 B**

As the royalty relates to every unit produced, it is therefore classified as a direct expense.

**15 B**

Inventory is valued at full production cost.

**16 A**

Supervisor's wages are usually classified as a step cost because a supervisor may be responsible for supervising up to a specific number of workers. However, if output increases such that additional direct labour is required, then an extra supervisor will be required.

| | |
|---|---|
| 1 – 10 workers | 1 supervisor |
| 11 – 20 workers | 2 supervisors |

**17 C**

C is the correct answer because a manager is not a cost object but may be linked to a cost centre in a responsibility accounting system.

**18 B**

Answers A and C are both incorrect, leaving B as the only possible answer. Depreciation of fixtures is an overhead cost, and could be production, administration or selling and distribution overheads, depending on the nature of the fixtures.

**19 D**

The cost of the ingredients is a direct material cost.

**20 B**

The prime cost is the total of all direct costs which will include direct expenses as well as direct labour and materials.

**21 C**

The inventory valuation will be unchanged. Finished goods are valued at the total production cost and the rent is a distribution cost.

**22 A**

The graph shows a reduction in unit variable costs beyond certain output levels. Only Answer A is consistent with this cost behaviour pattern.

**23 B**

Managers are not usually classified as direct labour.

**24 C**

Item B describes the costs of an activity or cost centre. Item A describes cost units. Item D describes budget centres. A cost centre is defined as 'a production or service location, function, activity or item of equipment for which costs are accumulated'.

**25 C**

| | $ |
|---|---|
| Total cost of 18,500 hours | 251,750 |
| Total cost of 17,000 hours | 246,500 |
| Variable cost of 1,500 hours | 5,250 |

Variable cost per machine hour = $5,250/1,500 machine hours = $3.50.

| | $ |
|---|---|
| Total cost of 17,000 hours | 246,500 |
| Less variable cost of 17,000 hours (× $3.50) | 59,500 |
| Balance = fixed costs | 187,000 |

**26 A**

The cost is direct as it can be directly attributed to a job. It is an expense because it is invoiced to the company and not a payroll cost.

**27 A**

| | *Cost per unit ($)* *(125 units)* | *Cost per unit ($)* *(180 units)* |
|---|---|---|
| T1 | 8.00 | 7.00 |
| T2 | 14.00 | 14.00 |
| T3 | 19.80 | 15.70 |
| T4 | 25.80 | 25.80 |

Cost types T2 and T4 are variable and T1 and T3 are semi-variable.

**28 A**

| | $ |
|---|---|
| Total cost of 15,100 square metres | 83,585 |
| Total cost of 12,750 square metres | 73,950 |
| Variable cost of 2,350 square metres | 9,635 |

Variable cost is $9,635/2,350 square metres = $4.10 per square metre.

Fixed costs can be found by substitution:

| | $ |
|---|---|
| Total cost of 12,750 square metres | 73,950 |
| Variable cost of 12,750 square metres (× $4.10) | 52,275 |
| Fixed costs | 21,675 |

So for 16,200 square metres:

Overheads = $21,675 + (16,200 × $4.10)

= $88,095

**29 A**

**30 B**

| | $ |
|---|---|
| Total cost of 10,000 units | 400,000 |
| Total cost of 5,000 units | 250,000 |
| Variable cost of 5,000 units | 150,000 |

Therefore the variable cost per unit = $150,000/5,000 units = $30 per unit.

**31 C**

| | units | | $ |
|---|---|---|---|
| Total cost of | 20,000 | = | 40,000 |
| Total cost of | 4,000 | = | 20,000 |
| Therefore variable cost of | 16,000 | = | 20,000 |

Variable cost per unit = $20,000/16,000 units = $1.25 per unit.

**32 A**

As advertising will hopefully generate sales, advertising is the independent variable and sales revenue the dependent; i.e. advertising is x and sales revenue is y.

| | | $ |
|---|---|---|
| High | Sales revenue from $6,500 of advertising | 225,000 |
| Low | Sales revenue from $2,500 of advertising | 125,000 |
| | Marginal sales revenue from $4,000 of advertising | 100,000 |

Marginal sales revenue for each $1 of advertising = $100,000/$4,000 = $25.

| | $ |
|---|---|
| Sales revenue from $6,500 of advertising | 225,000 |
| Marginal sales revenue from $6,500 of advertising (× $25) | 162,500 |
| Fixed sales revenue (even with no advertising) | 62,500 |

This gives a function of sales revenue = $62,500 + $25x, where x is the spending on advertising.

**33 C**

In the formula C = 1,000 + 250P, 1,000 represents the weekly fixed costs and 250 the variable cost per unit.

**34 B**

C= F + Vx

14,520 = 7,788 + V(3,300)

6,732= 3,300V

V= 2.04

**35 D**

Graph D is consistent with the cost behaviour for total materials given.

Graph A implies that there is a certain range of activity (just above 15,000 units) when total materials cost is constant.

Graph B implies that total materials cost falls beyond 15,000 units of activity.

Graph C implies that the lower cost per unit for materials applies only to units purchased in excess of 15,000.

**36 A**

For the first 10 hours of calls only the fixed line rental is charged therefore the answer cannot be B or D, which show no costs until a number of hours have passed. Graph C shows a variable cost is charged from nil to a maximum number of hours which is incorrect. The answer is A.

**37 C**

Use the two levels of production above 1,100 units per month for the high-low analysis as at these levels fixed costs are the same.

| *Units* | *Total cost* ($) |
|---|---|
| 1,400 | 68,200 |
| 1,200 | 66,600 |
| 200 | 1,600 |

Variable cost per unit = ($1,600 ÷ 200) = $8

Total fixed cost (above 1,100 units) = [$68,200 – (1,400 × $8)] = $57,000

Total cost for 1,000 units = [($57,000 – $6,000) + (1,000 × $8)] = $59,000

# BUSINESS MATHEMATICS

**38 A**

The question stated that there were just three possible outcomes for profit in a decision situation. The requirement asked for the most likely level of profits, that is the one of the three possibilities with the highest probability of occurring. The probability of a $28,500 profit was 0.40 ($11,400 / $28,500) and that of a $18,000 profit was 0.45 ($8,100 / $18,500).

**39 A**

[(180,000 x 1) + (75,000 x 2)] ÷ [1+2] = $110,000

B is incorrect – the approach here has weighted the two profits equally and notin the ratio described in the question.

**40 A**

The most likely level of profit is the one of the three possibilities with the highest probability of occurring – that of a $16,000 profit was 0.50 (8,000 ÷ 16,000).

**41 A**

Coefficient of determination = $r^2 = 0.6 \times 0.6 = 0.36 = 36\%$

**42 B**

$$a = \frac{\sum y}{n} - \frac{b\sum x}{n}$$

$$a = \frac{183.0}{5} - \frac{4.2(21)}{5} = [36.6 - 17.64] = 18.96.$$

If there are 5 salesmen in the month, expected costs will be, in $000:

18.96 + (4.2 × 5) = **39.96**.

**43 A**

This question is a simple test of your understanding of the meaning of the elements in a regression analysis formula. Statements (i) and (ii) are correct, but statement (iii) is wrong. The total value of x multiplied by the total value of y would be written as $\Sigma x\ \Sigma y$, not as $\Sigma xy$.

**44 B**

You should use the formulae provided in the examination (formulae sheet)

$$b = \frac{11 \times 13{,}467 - (440 \times 330)}{(11 \times 17{,}986) - (440)^2} = \frac{2{,}937}{4{,}246} = 0.6917$$

**45 B**

$\Sigma x$ = Σ Advertising expenditure = 100,000

$\Sigma y$ = Σ Sales revenue = 600,000

n = number of pairs of data = 5

**46 B**

$\Sigma y$ = 17,500 + 19,500 + 20,500 + 18,500 + 17,000 = 93,000

$\Sigma x$ = 300 + 360 + 400 + 320 + 280 = 1,660

a = (93,000 ÷ 5) – 29.53(1,660 ÷ 5) = 8,796.04

**47 B**

+1 represents perfect positive correlation.

–1 represents perfect negative correlation.

The nearer to 0 the correlation coefficient the less correlation between the variables.

**48 A**

Expected profits:

For W = $30,000

For X = $15,000

For Y = $26,000

For Z = $27,000

**49 D**

Sales rep A ($40,000 × 0.3) + ($60,000 × 0.4) + ($80,000 × 0.3) = $60,000

Sales rep B ($40,000 × 0.2) + ($60,000 × 0.7) + ($80,000 × 0.1) = $58,000

Sales rep C ($40,000 × 0.3) + ($60,000 × 0.5) + ($80,000 × 0.2) = $58,000

Sales rep D ($40,000 × 0.3) + ($60,000 × 0.3) + ($80,000 × 0.4) = $62,000

The highest expected sales revenue is from sales rep D.

**50 C**

Expected return = (0.1 × 13) + (0.65 × 8) + (0.25 × 5) = 7.75%.

**Answer D** is the **most likely** (normal) return

**Answer B** is a **simple average** of the returns

**Answer A** is the mid point return i.e. ½ (13 + 5)

**51 A**

$$b = \frac{n\Sigma xy - \Sigma x \Sigma y}{n\Sigma x^2 - (\Sigma x)^2}$$

$$= [(5 \times 23{,}091) - (129 \times 890)] \div [(5 \times 3{,}433) - (129^2)] = 1.231$$

$$a = \frac{\Sigma y}{n} - b\frac{\Sigma x}{n}$$

$$= (890 \div 5) - [(1.231 \times 129) \div 5] = 146 \text{ (nearest whole number)}$$

**52 B**

The correlation coefficient must be between +1 and –1.

## ORDERING AND ACCOUNTING FOR INVENTORY

### 53 C

{[Buffer Inventory + (EOQ ÷2)] × Annual holding cost per component}

= [700 units + (1500 units÷2)] × €3.00 = €4,350

### 54 C

Materials inventory account

| | $000s | | $000s |
|---|---|---|---|
| Opening inventory | 15 | Issued to production | 165 |
| Payables for purchases | 176 | Returned to suppliers | 8 |
| Returned to stores | 9 | Written off | 4 |
| | | Closing balance (balancing item) | 23 |
| | 200 | | 200 |

### 55 D

Option A: A stores ledger account records details of receipts and issues

Option B: A stores requisition will also detail quantity required

Option C: Lead time is the time between placing an order and receiving goods

### 56 B

Continuous stocktaking is being described. Perpetual inventory involves recording, as they occur, receipts, issues and the resulting balances of individual items of inventory, in either quantity, or quantity and value.

### 57 B

Indirect materials are overhead costs so debit production overhead. An issue of materials is a credit from the material control account

### 58 C

A purchase order will be raised by the stores department and sent to the supplier.

**59 A**

Materials inventory account

| | $000s | | $000s |
|---|---|---|---|
| Opening inventory | 23 | Issued to production | 144 |
| Purchases (bal fig) | 131 | | |
| Returned to stores | 5 | | |
| | | Closing balance (balancing item) | 15 |
| | 159 | | 159 |

**60 B**

Standard costs are used to help control the costs of purchases. Regular stocktakes and physical security help to minimise losses from stores.

# ORDER QUANTITIES AND REORDER LEVELS

**61 A**

The formula for the EOQ has the holding cost as the denominator. If this increases, the EOQ will be lower. A lower EOQ means that more orders will have to be placed each year; therefore, the total annual ordering cost will increase.

**62 C**

| | | $ |
|---|---|---|
| Purchase costs | (20,000 units × $40) | 800,000 |
| Order costs | (20,000/500 orders × $25/order) | 1,000 |
| Holding costs | (500/2 average units × $4/unit) | 1,000 |
| Total costs | | 802,000 |

**63 C**

Maximum usage × maximum lead time = 520 × 15 = 7,800 units

**64 B**

Average inventory = ROQ/2 + minimum inventory

= 100/2 + 20 = 70 chairs

**65 D**

The economic batch quantity determines the batch size for products manufactured internally. The EBQ is the batch size which minimises the total of inventory holding costs and batch set-up costs.

**66 B**

**Economic batch quantity** = $\sqrt{\dfrac{2C_oD}{C_h\left(1-\dfrac{D}{R}\right)}}$

$= \sqrt{\dfrac{2(1{,}500)(40{,}000)}{25\left(1-\dfrac{40{,}000}{100{,}000}\right)}}$

$= \sqrt{\dfrac{120\text{million}}{15}}$

$= \sqrt{8{,}000{,}000}$

= 2,828 units.

**67 A**

The EOQ model distinguishes between holding costs (i and ii) and ordering costs (iii)

**68 C**

Annual holding cost = {[Buffer inventory + (EOQ ÷2)] x Annual holding cost per component}

= {[500 + (2000 ÷2)] x2} = 3,000

**69 A**

Let O = ordering cost

185 = √{[ 2 × O × (4 × 2,000) ] ÷ [0.05 × 42]}

185 = √(16,000 × O ÷ 2.1)

O = $185^2$ × 2.1 ÷ 16,000 = $4.49

Note that the period for demand must be the same as that given for holding cost. As holding cost is given as an annual figure quarterly demand must be converted to annual demand by multiplying by 4.

**70 C**

Using the formula given: EOQ = √[(2 × 120 × 48,000) ÷ (0.10 × 80)] = 1,200 units

**71 A**

| | $ |
|---|---|
| Purchasing cost (48,000 × $80) | 3,840,000 |
| Ordering cost (48,000 ÷ 1,200) × $120 | 4,800 |
| Holding costs [(1,200 ÷ 2) × $80 × 0.10] | 4,800 |
| Total cost | 3,849,600 |

**72 C**

| | $ |
|---|---|
| Purchasing cost (48,000 × \$80 × 0.99) | 3,801,600 |
| Ordering cost (48,000 ÷ 2,000) × \$120 | 2,880 |
| Holding costs [(2,000 ÷ 2) × \$80 × 0.99 × 0.10] | 7,920 |
| Total cost | 3,812,400 |

Annual total saving = \$(3,849,600 – 3,812,400) \$37,200

**73 C**

| Order quantity = 750 units | | $ | Order quantity = 2,000 units | | $ |
|---|---|---|---|---|---|
| Order cost | 600 × 12 × 8.75/750 = | 84 | Order cost | 600 × 12 × 8.75/2,000 = | 31.50 |
| Holding cost | 0.1 × 2.24 × 750/2 = | 84 | Holding cost | 0.1 × 2.24 × 0.95 × 2,000/2 = | 212.80 |
| Purchase cost | 600 × 12 × 2.24 = | 16,12 | Purchase cost | 600 × 12 × 2.24 × 0.95 = | 15,321.60 |
| Total cost | | 16,29 | | | 15,565.90 |

Change in cost = \$16,296 – \$15,566 = saving of \$730.

**74 C**

Annual production rate = 500 × 50 = 25,000

Using the economic batch quantity formula given,

2,000 = √{(2 × setup cost × 5,000)/(1.5 × (1-5,000/25,000))}

Setup cost = 2000 × 2000 × 1.5 × 0.8/(2 × 5,000) = \$480

# ACCOUNTING FOR LABOUR

**75 A**

Statement (i) is correct, because extra spending would be incurred to pay the additional temporary staff. Statement (ii) is incorrect, because total spending on labour is unaffected when spare capacity is utilised and idle time reduced. Statement (iii) is also incorrect, because total labour costs will not be increased by switching labour from working on one product to working on another product. However, there is an opportunity cost in switching labour. This is the total contribution forgone by no longer producing and selling the original product. This opportunity cost would be a relevant cost in evaluating a decision to switch the labour from one product to the other. Even so, as worded, statement (iii) is incorrect.

**76 B**

Unless the overtime can be traced to a specific product or job, it will be treated as an indirect production cost and absorbed into units using the normal absorption basis.

**77 B**

The employee took 44 hours to perform 94 operations. The standard time allowed per operation is 37.5 minutes, giving a standard time of (94 × [37.5/60]) = 58.75 hours to perform 94 operations. The time saved is therefore (58.75 – 44) = 14.75 hours. The bonus payable will be:

(time taken/time allowed) × time saved × hourly rate

= (44/58.75) × 14.75 × \$6.50 = \$71.80 (rounded).

The gross wage for Week 24 will therefore be (44 hours × \$6.50) + \$71.80 = \$357.80.

**78 A**

Direct labour costs are credited to wages and salaries and debited to work-in-progress.

**79 D**

\$240,000 ÷0.80 = \$300,000

**80 C**

If direct labour is working at below the agreed productivity level, this will lead to lower output than planned. This could have been caused by factors which resulted in idle time, such as (ii) and (iii) but would not lead to idle time.

**81 B**

40 × \$15 = \$600. Note that the basic element of overtime is classified as a direct cost. The normal treatment of overtime premium is for it to be treated as an indirect cost.

**82 B**

Average employment during the year was (5,250 + 5,680) / 2 = 5,465

The labour turnover rate = 360/5,465 × 100% = 6.6%

**83 D**

Expected hours to make actual output/actual hours = 192/180 × 100% = 106.7%

**84 D**

Actual hours/budget hours = 180/185 × 100% = 97.3%

**85 C**

Expected hours to make actual output/budget hours = 192/185 × 100% = 103.8%

# ACCOUNTING FOR OVERHEADS

**86 B**

Reapportion service cost centre K first as it does work for service cost centre J but not vice versa.

| | G | H | J | K |
|---|---|---|---|---|
| Overhead cost ($) | 40,000 | 50,000 | 30,000 | 18,000 |
| Reapportion K | 9,000 | 7,200 | 1,800 | (18,000) |
| | | | 31,800 | |
| Reapportion J | 9,540 | | (31,800) | |
| | $58,540 | | | |

**87 C**

An absorption rate is used to determine the full cost of a product or service. Answer A describes overhead allocation and apportionment. Absorption does not control overheads, so answer D is not correct.

**88 D**

P = 95,000 + 0.4X + 0.3Y

X = 46,000 + 0.1Y

Y = 30,000 + 0.2X

X = 46,000 + 0.1(30,000 + 0.2X) = 46,000 + 3,000 + 0.02X

0.98X = 49,000 and X = 50,000

Y = 30,000 + 0.2(50,000) = 40,000

P = 95,000 + 0.4(50,000) + 0.3(40,000) = 127,000

Alternatively use the repeated distribution method as follows;

| | P | Q | X | Y |
|---|---|---|---|---|
| Overhead cost ($) | 95,000 | 82,000 | 46,000 | 30,000 |
| Reapportion X | 18,400 | 18,400 | (46,000) | 9,200 |
| Reapportion Y | 11,760 | 23,520 | 3,920 | (39,200) |
| Reapportion X | 1,568 | 1,568 | (3,920) | 784 |
| Reapportion Y | 235 | 470 | 78 | (784) |
| Reapportion X | 31 | 31 | (78) | 16 |
| Reapportion Y | 5 | 9 | 2 | (16) |
| Rounding | 1 | 1 | | |
| | $127,000 | | | |

**89 B**

| | $ |
|---|---|
| Actual expenditure | 56,389 |
| Absorbed cost (12,400 × 1.02 × $4.25) | 53,754 |
| Total under-absorption | 2,635 |

**90 A**

Under- or over-absorption is determined by comparing the actual overhead expenditure with the overhead absorbed.

**91 D**

Fixed production overheads are over-absorbed when actual expenditure is less than budget and/or actual production volume is higher than budget.

**92 D**

Over-absorbed overheads increase profit, and so are recorded as a credit entry in either an over-absorbed overhead account or directly as a credit in the income statement. The matching debit entry could be either in the WIP account or the production overhead control account, depending on the costing system used.

**93 C**

Indirect labour is a costing concept. The double entry is:

**Wages control**

| | |
|---|---|
| | Indirect labour × (overheads) |

**Overhead control**

| | |
|---|---|
| Indirect labour × (wages) | |

**94 A**

| | | |
|---|---|---|
| Machining hours | = | (4,000 × 0.5 hour) + (4,000 × 1.0 hour) |
| | = | 6,000 hours |
| Assembly hours | = | (4,000 × 0.2 hour) + (4,000 × 0.25 hour) |
| | = | 1,800 hours |
| Machining absorption rate | = | $\frac{\$120,000}{6,000 \text{ hours}}$ |
| | = | $20 per hour |
| Assembly absorption rate | = | $\frac{\$72,000}{1,800 \text{ hours}}$ |
| | = | $40 per hour |
| Fixed overhead per unit of Pye | = | (0.5 hour × $20) + (0.2 hour × $40) |
| | = | $18 |

**95 D**

Cost apportionment is concerned with sharing costs according to benefit received.

**96 B**

| | $ |
|---|---|
| Actual overheads | 694,075 |
| Under recovery | (35,000) |
| Overhead absorbed | 659,075 |

$$OAR = \frac{\$659{,}075}{32{,}150} = \$20.50$$

**97 B**

| | $ |
|---|---|
| Actual overheads | 245,600 |
| Over-absorption of overheads | 6,400 |
| Overheads absorbed | 252,000 |

Absorption rate = $252,000/45,000 hours = $5.60 per direct labour hour.

**98 D**

| | $ |
|---|---|
| Actual overhead | 138,000 |
| Over-absorbed overhead | 23,000 |
| Therefore amount of overhead absorbed | 161,000 |

Hours worked = 11,500.

Therefore absorption rate per hour = $161,000/11,500 hours = $14 per hour.

**99 C**

Let the overhead apportioned from service department C be $C.

Let the overhead apportioned from service department D be $D.

C = 3,200 + 0.20D .....(1)

D = 4,600 + 0.10 C ....(2)

Substitute (1) in (2)

D = 4,600 + 0.10(3,200 + 0.20D)

D = 4,600 + 320 + 0.02D

$0.98D = 4{,}920$

$D = 5{,}020.$

Substitute in (1)

$C = 3{,}200 + 0.20\,(5{,}020)$

$C = 4{,}204.$

Total overhead for department X = 5,000 + 0.50C + 0.20D

= 5,000 + 0.50(4,204) + 0.20 (5,020)

= 5,000 + 2,102 + 1,004

= 8,106.

Allowing for a rounding difference, this is answer C.

***Note:*** You could have reached the same answer by using the repeated distribution method.

**100 B**

Fixed overhead absorption rate = \$36,000/18,000 = \$2 per direct labour hour.

Variable overhead absorption rate = \$9,000/18,000 = \$0.50 per direct labour hour.

| | \$ | \$ |
|---|---|---|
| Overheads absorbed: | | |
| Fixed (20,000 × \$2) | | 40,000 |
| Variable (20,000 × \$0.50) | | 10,000 |
| Total overhead absorbed | | 50,000 |
| Overheads incurred: | | |
| Fixed | 39,000 | |
| Variable | 12,000 | |
| Total overhead incurred | | 51,000 |
| Under-absorbed overhead | | 1,000 |

**101 B**

$(\$3{,}000 \times \frac{700}{8{,}000}) + (\$11{,}000 \times \frac{80}{400}) + (\$7{,}000 \times \frac{20}{70})$ = \$(262.50 + 2,200 + 2,000) = \$4,462.50

**102 C**

$$\$12 \times \frac{60}{120} + \$8 \times \frac{100}{100} = \$14$$

# MARGINAL AND ABSORPTION COSTING

**103 C**

| | |
|---|---|
| Total variable cost | = \$(4 + 5 + 3 + 3) = \$15 |
| Contribution per unit | = \$20 – \$15 = \$5 |
| Total contribution earned | = \$5 × 800 = \$4,000 |

**104 D**

The distance between the profit/loss line and the fixed cost line represents contribution.

**105 D**

Contribution per unit = (\$24 ÷ 0.60 × 0.40) = \$16

Breakeven point = (\$720,000 ÷ \$16) = 45,000 units

**106 D**

If a sales value of \$100 per unit is assumed then the original and revised situations will be:

| | *Original* | *Revised* |
|---|---|---|
| | \$ | \$ |
| Selling price | 100 | 110 |
| Variable cost/unit | 60 | 60 |
| Contribution/unit | 40 | 50 |

Fixed costs do not affect contribution and if sales volume is unchanged then the overall change in contribution can be measured using the contribution per unit:

$$\frac{(50-40)}{40} = 25\%$$

**107 D**

Absorption costing profit = \$2,000 > Marginal Costing profit = \$(3,000)

Therefore Production > Sales by \$5,000

\$5,000 = OAR x number of units change in stock

\$5,000 = \$2 x number of units change in stock

Therefore number of units change in stock = $\frac{\$5,000}{\$2}$ = 2,500

If Sales = 10,000 units, therefore Production = Sales + 10,000 units = 12,500 units.

**108 B**

Contribution per unit = $(10 – 6) = $4.

| | $ |
|---|---|
| Total contribution (250,000 × $4) | 1,000,000 |
| Fixed overheads (200,000 × $2) | 400,000 |
| Profit | 600,000 |

**109 B**

Fixed production overhead per unit = $48,000/12,000 units = $4.

Sales volume is less than production volume by 280 units.

In absorption costing, this means that some fixed overheads will be carried forward in the closing inventory value. Fixed overheads in this addition to inventory = 280 units × $4 = $1,120.

In marginal costing, all fixed overheads incurred in a period are charged as an expense against profit. Marginal costing profit would therefore be lower than the absorption costing profit by $1,120.

**110 B**

As inventory decreases over the period, the cost of sales will be higher with absorption costing, since they will include fixed overhead in the opening inventory now sold. The extra cost of sales (and thus reduction in profit) = (8,500 – 6,750) × $3 = $5,250.

This means that since profit will be lower with absorption costing by $5,250, the absorption costing profit will be $(62,100 – 5,250) = $56,850.

**111 C**

There was an increase in inventory in the period; therefore the absorption costing profit is higher than the marginal costing profit (because a larger amount of fixed overhead is carried forward in the closing inventory value).

| | $ |
|---|---|
| Marginal costing profit | 72,300 |
| *Less:* fixed costs in opening inventory (300 units × $5) | (1,500) |
| *Add:* fixed costs in closing inventory (750 units × $5) | 3,750 |
| Absorption costing profit | 74,550 |

**112 B**

Production volume exceeded sales volume, so the profit with absorption costing is higher than the profit with marginal costing.

Fixed overheads in inventory = $30,000/750 = $40 per unit, therefore total fixed overhead in closing inventory (absorption costing) = 250 units × $40 = $10,000. Profit with marginal costing is therefore lower by $10,000.

**113 D**

| | $ |
|---|---|
| Sales revenue (600 × ($90,000/500 per unit)) | 108,000 |
| Production cost of sales (600 × ($75,000/750)) | 60,000 |
| | 48,000 |
| Under-absorbed overhead (750 – 700 units) × $40 | 2,000 |
| | 46,000 |
| Variable selling costs (600 × ($5,000/500)) | 6,000 |
| Fixed selling costs | 25,000 |
| Profit | 15,000 |

**114 B**

The marginal cost of a product is the additional cost of producing an extra unit and is therefore the sum of the variable costs. If the inventory increases over a year, absorption costing profit will be higher than marginal costing profit because an element of fixed cost will be carried forward in closing inventory to be charged against profit in a future period.

**115 A**

Although there is a 'kink' in the total cost line, this is due to a step increase in total fixed costs. Variable unit costs are the same at all levels of output and sales, because the slope of the total cost line is unchanged.

**116 C**

| | |
|---|---|
| Contribution per unit $(60 – 15 – 5) | $40 |
| Total fixed costs ($30 × 2,400) | $72,000 |
| Breakeven point ($72,000 ÷ $40 per unit) | 1,800 units |

**117 B**

In an absorption costing system, the fixed cost per unit would be $3,000/15,000 units = $0.20 per unit.

Budgeted profit with marginal costing = Contribution – Fixed costs

= $26,000 – $3,000 = $23,000.

By switching to absorption costing, in a period when inventory levels increase by 2,000 units, absorption costing profit would be higher by 2,000 units × fixed cost per unit, i.e. by 2,000 × $0.20 = $400.

Absorption costing profit = $23,000 + $400 = $23,400.

**118 A**

Total contribution will increase as sales volume increases, but the contribution per unit will be constant as long as the sales price and variable cost per unit are unchanged. Overhead is not absorbed to product unit so there is no under/over absorption of overhead. Marginal costing does provide useful information for decision making because it highlights contribution, which is a relevant cash flow for decision-making purposes.

**119 C**

Budgeted profit = $125,000

Budgeted profit/unit = $1

Therefore budgeted sales = 125,000 units.

Budgeted fixed costs = 125,000 units × $4 = $500,000.

Contribution/unit = $8 – $3 = $5.

Breakeven point = $500,000/$5 = 100,000 units.

Margin of safety = 125,000 – 100,000 = 25,000 units.

Margin of safety is normally measured as a percentage of the budgeted sales, which in this case is 25,000/125,000 = 0.20 or 20%.

**120 C**

The diagram shows that at an activity level of $500,000 worth of sales, the profit was $140,000.It also shows that the loss at zero activity is $60,000 which also represents the total fixed costs. Therefore :

Contribution at $500,000 of sales is =$200,000 (140,000 + 60,000)

Contribution to sales ratio =[200,000 ÷ 500,000 x 100] = 40%

**121 C**

During the period, inventory increased by 34,000 – 31,000 = 3,000 units.

Fixed overhead in the additional closing inventory = $(955,500 – 850,500) = $105,000.

Fixed overhead per unit = $105,000/3,000 = $35 per unit.

Budgeted fixed costs = $1,837,500.

Budgeted production volume = $1,837,500/$35 per unit = 52,500 units.

**122 C**

Breakeven number of units = $\dfrac{\text{Fixed costs}}{\text{Contribution per unit}}$

If the selling price per unit and the variable cost per unit both rise by 10%, then the contribution per unit also rises by 10%.

Given no change in fixed costs, the breakeven number of units will therefore decrease.

**123 D**

Contribution per unit = $27

Contribution to sales ratio = 45%

Selling price = $27 ÷ 0.45 = $60

Margin of safety in units = $13,500 ÷ $60 = 225

Breakeven point (BEP) = 1,000 – 225 = 775 units

At BEP: total contribution = total fixed costs

Total fixed costs = 775 × $27 = $20,925

**124 C**

Contribution per unit (CPU) = $(80 – 30 – 10) = $40

Total fixed cost = 2,880 × $25 = $72,000

Breakeven point = $72,000 ÷ $40 = 1,800 units.

**125 A**

Breakeven point in sales revenue= Fixed costs / Contribution to sales ratio

= $48,000 / 40% = $120,000.

If actual sales revenue = $140,000, then the margin of safety is $20,000 ($140,000 – $120,000) in terms of sales revenue.

Since the selling price is $10 per unit, this is equivalent to 2,000 units.

**126 B**

| | |
|---|---|
| Contribution per unit | = 0.40 × $60 = $24 |
| Breakeven point | = $54,000 ÷ $24 = 2,250 units |
| Margin of safety | = 4,000 – 2,250 = 1,750 units |

**127 B**

From the chart BEP = 1,200 units

3,000/contribution per unit = 1,200 so contribution per unit = $2.50

1,700 × 2.50 = $4,250

**128 B**

| | |
|---|---|
| Contribution per unit | = $26 – $10 = $16. |
| Breakeven point | = $50,000/$16 per unit = 3,125 units. |

**129 A**

Breakeven = 80% of 5,000 units = 4,000 units.

Total contribution at 4,000 units = (4,000 × $25) = $100,000.

Profit at 4,000 units = $0.

Fixed costs are therefore $100,000.

**130 A**

Profit figures only differ if inventory changes in the period.

**131 C**

Point C is where total revenue exceeds total costs by the largest amount, i.e. where profit is maximised.

**132 C**

Line A is total revenue

Line B is total cost

Line D is fixed cost

**133 B**

Suppose we start with the following situation.

| | *\$ per unit* |
|---|---|
| Selling price | 100 |
| Variable cost | (60) |
| Contribution | 40 |

Sales 1,000 units; total contribution \$40,000

A, B and C would have the following effects.

| | *A* | *B* |
|---|---|---|
| | *\$ per unit* | *\$ per unit* |
| Selling price | 100 | 110 |
| Variable cost | (54) | (60) |
| Contribution | 46 | 50 |
| Total contribution | \$46,000 | \$50,000 |

C : Total contribution = \$40,000 × 1.1

= \$44,000

Fixed costs are irrelevant since we are concerned with *contribution.*

**134 B**

Inventory is valued at full production cost i.e. both fixed and variable production costs.

\$(33.00 + 45.10) = \$78.10

**135 C**

The dotted line represents the level of fixed cost. The distance between the fixed cost line and the profit line represents the total contribution at any level of output.

**136 B**

Contribution per unit = $15 × 0.4 = $6

Breakeven point = $18,000 ÷ $15 = 1,200 units

Profit when 1,500 units sold = (1,500 – 1,200) × $6 = $1,800

Or FC/0.4 = $18,000 so FC = $7,200

Profit = 1,500 × 6 – 7,200 = $1,800

**137 C**

$$\text{Breakeven point} = \frac{\text{fixed costs}}{\text{C/S ratio}}$$

| | $ |
|---|---|
| Budgeted contribution | 200,000 |
| Budgeted profit | 50,000 |
| Therefore budgeted fixed costs | 150,000 |

Contribution/sales ratio = $200,000/$500,000 = 0.40.

$$\text{Breakeven point} = \frac{\$150{,}000}{0.40} = \$375{,}000$$

# RELEVANT COSTING

**138 B**

Relevant costs are future cash flows arising as a direct consequence of a decision. Items A and D are sunk costs, because they have already been incurred. Item C is a non-cash item of cost. Only item B is a relevant cost.

**139 B**

Materials can have an alternative use that can exceed their value in the project being considered.

**140 A**

250 hours at [$9 per hour + the opportunity cost $(12 ÷ 3) per hour] = $3,250

The incremental labour cost of weekend working is $4,500 (250 × $18) and being higher than $3,250 is therefore not relevant.

**141 A**

| | |
|---|---|
| Fall in scrap value | $500 |
| Cost of adjustments | $800 |
| Relevant cost | $1,300 |

**142 C**

The relevant value of a fixed asset is the higher of its net realisable value from disposal ($11,000) and its economic value in use ($17,500).

The historical cost is irrelevant. The asset would not be replaced, because replacement cost is more than the asset is worth to the business. The opportunity cost of the asset is the value of its most profitable alternative use, which is on the project to earn $17,500.

**143 C**

The relevant cost of labour is the lower cost of (1) the cost of working overtime and (2) the cost of diverting labour from other work.

Incremental cost of working overtime:

| | $ |
|---|---|
| Incremental cost of using 400 hours spare capacity | 0 |
| Incremental cost of overtime: 100 hours × $12 × 150% | 1,800 |
| | 1,800 |

Incremental cost of diverting labour from other work

| | $ |
|---|---|
| Labour cost: 100 hours × $12 | 1,200 |
| Contribution forgone: 100 hours × $2 | 200 |
| | 1,400 |

It would be cheaper to divert labour from other work, and the relevant cost is $1,400.

**144 B**

| Material | $ |
|---|---|
| T (500 × $45) | 22,500 |
| V (200 × $40) + (200 × $52) | 18,400 |
| Total relevant cost | 40,900 |

**145 D**

4,000 × [($20,000 ÷ 2,500) × 1.025] = $32,800

**146 A**

Lower of 350 × 12 = $4,200

and 350/7 × 14 + 350 × 8 = $3,500

**147 C**

The existing product uses $20/$8 = 2.5 hours to generate $25 contribution. The rate of contribution is therefore $10 per hour. Since skilled labour is in short supply the relevant cost of the contract is the wage rate plus the opportunity cost per hour.

Opportunity cost per skilled labour hour = contribution forgone = $10

| Relevant cost: | $ |
|---|---|
| Skilled labour cost (90 × $8) | 720 |
| Opportunity cost (90 × $10) | 900 |
| | 1,620 |

**148 C**

Relevant cost of a regularly used material in inventory is its replacement cost (600 × $27) = $16,200

**149 D** Opportunity cost now + disposal cost at end of contract = $(2,000 + 800) = $2,800

# DEALING WITH LIMITING FACTORS

**150 A**

The monthly shortfall is calculated by comparing the number of machine hours required to produce sufficient units for maximum monthly demand to the actual number of machine hours available.

Monthly machining hours required to meet maximum demand:

| *Product* | *Units* | *Hours/unit* | *Total hours* |
|---|---|---|---|
| R | 9,000 | (40 ÷ 60) = 0.667 | 6,000 |
| S | 6,000 | (54 ÷ 60) = 0.900 | 5,400 |
| T | 3,000 | (75 ÷ 60) = 1.250 | 3,750 |
| | | | 15,150 |
| Available hours | | | 10,500 |
| Shortfall in machining hours | | | 4,650 |

**151 C**

As there is only one limiting factor, the optimum monthly production plan is found by calculating the contribution per machine hour and ranking the results. The products are then produced in order until all of the available machine hours are used. Note that contribution is found using the c/s ratio. A c/s ratio of 20% means that for every $1 of sales revenue contribution is 20c.

Calculation of the contribution per machining hour for each product:

| | *R* | *S* | *T* |
|---|---|---|---|
| Selling price per unit | $60 | $75 | $84 |
| Contribution to sales ratio | 20% | 24% | 25% |
| Contribution per unit | $12 | $18 | $21 |
| Machining hours per unit | 0.667 | 0.900 | 1.250 |
| Contribution per machine hour | $18 | $20 | $16.80 |
| Ranking | 2nd | 1st | 3rd |

Optimal production plan:

| *Product* | *Units* | *Machine hours used* |
|---|---|---|
| S | 6,000 | 5,400 |
| R | 7,650 | 5,100 (balance) |
| Total | | 10,500 |

**152 B**

| *Product* | *Units* | *Contribution* ($) |
|---|---|---|
| S | 6,000 | 108,000 |
| R | 7,650 | 91,800 |
| Total | | 199,800 |

**153 C**

Objective function (maximisation of contribution) = 4X + Y

Let 4X + Y = 40,000 (assumed)

When X = 0, Y = 40,000

When Y = 0, X = 10,000

These two points are plotted on the graph and joined by a (dotted) line. This line is then moved away from the origin keeping it parallel to the originally drawn dotted line until it reaches the furthest most point in the feasible area (OHJKL).

In this case that will be the point K which is optimal.

**154 A**

10X + 7Y = 70,000

When X = 0, Y = 10,000

When Y = 0, X = 7,000

Constraint line (2) joins these two points on the axes.

**155 D**

Material required to meet maximum demand:

| | |
|---|---|
| 6,000 × (13 ÷ 4) + 8,000 × (19 ÷ 4) = | 57,500 litres |
| Material available: | 50,000 litres |

∴ Material is a limiting factor

Labour required to meet maximum demand:

| | |
|---|---|
| 6,000 × (35 ÷ 7) + 8,000 × (28 ÷ 7) = | 62,000 hours |
| Labour available: | 60,000 hours |

∴ Labour is a limiting factor

**156 D**

| | *X* | *Y* |
|---|---|---|
| Contribution per unit | $10 | $36 |
| Contribution per kg | $4 | $6 |
| Ranking | 2nd | 1st |

| *Product* | *Units* | *Hours per unit* | *Hours* | |
|---|---|---|---|---|
| Y | 600 | 6 | 3,600 | |
| X | 560 | 2.50 | 1,400 | (balance) |
| | | | 5,000 | |

**157 B**

| | | kg |
|---|---|---|
| Product I | (2,000 units × 36/6 kg/unit) | 12,000 |
| Product II | (1,500 units × 24/6 kg/unit) | 6,000 |
| Product III | (4,000 units × 15/6 kg/unit) | 10,000 |
| Total materials required | | 28,000 |

## 158 D

Statement D is correct. Statement A is incorrect: products should be ranked according to the contribution they earn for each unit of limiting factor. Statement B is incorrect: linear programming is not required when there is only one limiting factor – products can simply be ranked according to the contribution they earn per unit of limiting factor. Statement C is incorrect, because the point furthest from the origin might not be in the feasible region.

## 159 C

Hours required to meet demand = (5,000 × 0.4) + (5,000 × 0.5) + (2,000 × 0.75) = 6,000 hours. Labour is therefore a limiting factor, since only 3,600 hours are available.

| | X | Y | Z |
|---|---|---|---|
| Contribution per unit | $24 | $25 | $30 |
| Hours per unit | 0.40 | 0.50 | 0.75 |
| Contribution per hour | $60 | $50 | $40 |
| Ranking | 1st | 2nd | 3rd |

| *Optimal plan* | *Units* | *Hours* |
|---|---|---|
| X | 5,000 | 2,000 |
| Y (balance: 1,600/0.50) | 3,200 | 1,600 |
| | | 3,600 |

## 160 C

Materials required to meet sales demand = 1,000 × (1 + 0.5 + 2) = 3,500 square metres.

Labour required = 1,000 × (3 + 1 + 1) = 5,000 hours.

Labour is a limiting factor but materials are not.

| | *Kilts* | *Skirts* | *Dresses* |
|---|---|---|---|
| Contribution per unit | $12 | $5.50 | $7 |
| Contribution per labour hour | $4 | $5.50 | $7 |
| Ranking | 3rd | 2nd | 1st |

Since only 1,000 hours are available, profit will be maximised by making 1,000 dresses.

## 161 A

2,000 kg of material G produces 100 units of product Y = 20 kg per unit

2,700 kg of material H produces 90 units of product Y = 30 kg per unit

**162 D**

2,000 kg of material G produces 125 units of product X = 16 kg per unit

2,700 kg of material H produces 150 units of product X = 18 kg per unit

The constraints are drawn on the graph as equalities and their intersection can be found using simultaneous equations

| | | |
|---|---|---|
| Equation 1 | 16X + 20Y = 2,000 | Material G |
| Equation 2 | 18X + 30Y = 2,700 | Material H |
| Equation 3 1 × 1.5 | 24X + 30Y = 3,000 | |
| Equation 3 – equation 2 | 6X = 300 so X = 50 | |

Input into equation 1 16 × 50 + 20Y = 2,000 Y = (2,000 – 800)/20 = 60

**163 D**

| Total contribution from: | $ |
|---|---|
| A 90 units of Y (90 × $12) | 1,080 |
| B 50 units of X + 60 units of Y (50 × $30) + (60 × $12) | 2,220 |
| C 60 units of X + 50 units of Y (60 × $30) + (50 × $12) | 2,400 |
| D 125 units of X (125 × $30) | 3,750 |

Optimal mix is the one giving the highest total contribution ($3,750)

**164 D**

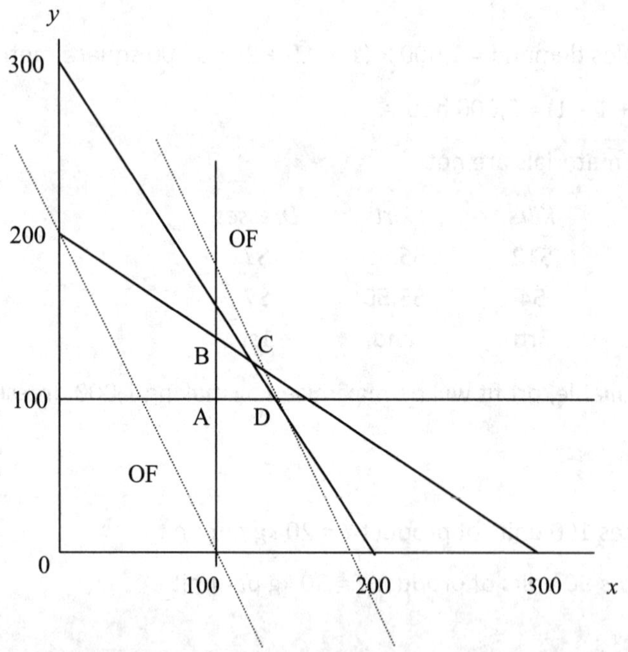


You might notice that the slope of the contribution line in the diagram in the question is steeper than the slope of the constraint line joining points C and D. It therefore follows that the outermost point in the feasible area that will give the optimal solution to the linear programming problem is point D rather than point C.

## 165 C

Since the company has an objective of **minimising** costs, the potential optimal solutions are those corner points of the feasible area that are closest to the origin of the graph, i.e. D and E.

## 166 B

Find the intersection by solving the simultaneous equations

Equation 1 $12.5X + 25Y = 1{,}375$

Equation 2 $17.5X + 20Y = 1{,}325$

Equation 1 $\times$ 1.4 $17.5X + 35Y = 1{,}925$ Equation 3

Equation 3 – equation 2 $15Y = 60$ so $Y = 40$

Insert into equation 1 $12.5X + 25 \times 40 = 1{,}375$

$X = (1{,}375 - 1{,}000)/12.5 = 30$

## 167 A

| *Product* | *X* | *Y* | *Z* |
|---|---|---|---|
| Contribution per unit | \$1.50 | \$1.60 | \$2.40 |
| Raw material required per unit | 0.3 kg | 0.4 kg | 0.8 kg |
| Contribution/per kg | \$5 | \$4 | \$3 |
| Rank | 1 | 2 | 3 |

| | |
|---|---|
| Make 4,000 X using | 1,200 kg |
| Next make 3,000 Y using | <u>1,200 kg</u> |
| | 2,400 kg |
| Remaining | 3,600 kg which is sufficient to make 3,600/0.8 = 4,500 kg of Z |

# JOB, BATCH AND PROCESS COSTING

**168 C**

| | Job 812 |
|---|---|
| | $ |
| Direct materials | 60 |
| Direct labour | 40 |
| Direct expenses | 20 |
| Prime cost | 120 |
| Production overheads ($40 ÷ 8) × $16 | 80 |
| Non-production overheads (0.6 × $120) | 72 |
| Total cost – Job 812 | 272 |

**169 D**

*Statement A* is correct. Job costs are identified with a particular job, whereas process costs (of units produced and work in process) are averages, based on equivalent units of production.

*Statement B* is also correct. The direct cost of a job to date, excluding any direct expenses, can be ascertained from materials requisition notes and job tickets or time sheets.

*Statement C* is correct, because without data about units completed and units still in process, losses and equivalent units of production cannot be calculated.

*Statement D* is incorrect, because the cost of normal loss will usually be incorporated into job costs as well as into process costs. In process costing this is commonly done by giving normal loss no cost, leaving costs to be shared between output, closing inventory and abnormal loss/gain. In job costing it can be done by adjusting direct materials costs to allow for normal wastage, and direct labour costs for normal reworking of items or normal spoilage.

**170 D**

| | *Job 1* | *Job 2* | *Total* |
|---|---|---|---|
| | $ | $ | $ |
| Opening WIP | 8,500 | 0 | 8,500 |
| Material in period | 17,150 | 29,025 | 46,175 |
| Labour for period | 12,500 | 23,000 | 35,500 |
| Overheads (see working) | 43,750 | 80,500 | 124,250 |
| | 81,900 | 132,525 | 214,425 |

***Working***

Total labour cost for period = $(12,500 + 23,000 + 4,500) = $40,000

Overhead absorption rate = $140,000/$40,000 = 3.5 times the direct labour cost.

**171 C**

| | *Job 3* |
|---|---|
| | $ |
| Opening WIP | 46,000 |
| Labour cost for period | 4,500 |
| Overheads (3.5 × $4,500) | 15,750 |
| Total production costs | 66,250 |
| Profit (50%) | 33,125 |
| Selling price of 2,400 boards | 99,375 |

Selling price of one board = $99,375/2,400 = $41.41

**172 D**

This can be calculated as a balancing figure in the process account.

**Process account**

| | kg | | $ | | kg | | $ |
|---|---|---|---|---|---|---|---|
| Input (balance) | 3,000 | | 21,150 | Output | 2,800 | (× 7.50) | 21,000 |
| Abnormal gain | 100 | (× 7.50) | 750 | Normal loss | 300 | (× 3) | 900 |
| | | | 21,900 | | | | 21,900 |

*Alternatively:*

| | $ |
|---|---|
| Cost of output (2,800 × 7.50) | 21,000 |
| Scrap value of normal loss (300 × 3) | 900 |
| | 21,900 |
| Less: Value of abnormal gain (100 × 7.50) | (750) |
| Cost of input | 21,150 |

**173 B**

| | *Units* |
|---|---|
| Input | 13,200 |
| Less: Normal loss (13,200 × 10/110) | 1,200 |
| Expected output | 12,000 |

| | $ |
|---|---|
| Process costs | 184,800 |
| Less: scrap value of normal loss (1,200 × $4) | 4,800 |
| Cost of good output | 180,000 |

Cost for each expected unit of output = $180,000/12,000 = $15.

Finished units of output, and also abnormal loss and abnormal gain units will be valued at this amount.

**174 B**

Cost per unit = net process costs/expected output

= (9,000 + 13,340 + 300)/ 2,000 -100

= $22,040/1,900 = $11.60.

**175 A**

| | $ |
|---|---|
| Opening WIP | 1,710 |
| Completion of opening WIP (300 × 0.40 × $10) | 1,200 |
| Units started and completed in the month | |
| (2,000 – 300) × $10 | 17,000 |
| Total value (2,000 units) | 19,910 |

**176 C**

| | *Materials equivalent units* |
|---|---|
| Opening inventory completed (400 × 0%) | 0 |
| Units started and finished in the period (800 – 400) | 400 |
| Closing inventory (600 × 75%) | 450 |
| Total equivalent units produced in the period | 850 |

**177 D**

Sales value of production :

Product W : (12,000 x 10) = $120,000
Product X : (10,000 x 12) = $120,000

Therefore joint production costs are apportioned W:X in the ratio 1:1
Amount apportioned to product X is (776,160 ÷2) = $388,080
20% of X's production is in closing inventory @ (0.2 x 388,080) = $77,616

Answer B has split the joint production costs on the basis of sales prices and Answer C has used the sales value of sales to apportion joint production costs.

**178 D**

| | Units |
|---|---|
| J: (6,000 – 100 + 300) = | 6,200 |
| K: (4,000 – 400 + 200) = | 3,800 |
| | 10,000 |

Joint costs apportioned to J: (6,200 ÷ 10,000) × \$110,000 = \$68,200

**179 C**

Total sales revenue = (\$18 × 10,000) + (\$25 × 20,000) + (\$20 × 20,000) = \$1,080,000

Joint costs to be allocated = \$277,000 – (\$2 × 3,500)

= \$270,000

Allocation rate = (\$270,000/1,080,000) = 0.25 of sales revenue.

Joint costs allocated to product 3 = 0.25 × (\$20 × 20,000)

= \$100,000

= (\$100,000/20,000 units) \$5 per unit

**180 C**

| | | \$ |
|---|---|---|
| Prime cost | | 6,840.00 |
| Fixed overhead | \$300,000/60,000 × 156 | 780.00 |
| | | 7,620.00 |
| Profit | 20% × 7,620.00 | 1,524.00 |
| Job price | | 9,144.00 |

**181 D**

Abnormal loss units are valued as one equivalent unit of cost, the same as units of good production. This cost is credited to the process account and debited to the abnormal loss account. The scrap value of abnormal loss is then credited to the abnormal loss account (with the matching debit to bank).

**182 A**

| | | kg |
|---|---|---|
| Input | | 12,750 |
| Output | Normal loss | 510 |
| | Finished goods | 12,700 |
| | | 13,210 |
| Abnormal gain | | 460 |

**183 A**

| | kg |
|---|---|
| Material input | 2,500 |
| Normal loss (10%) | (250) |
| Abnormal loss | (75) |
| Good production achieved | 2,175 |

**184 C**

Direct labour hours = \$400 ÷ \$8 = 50 hours

| | $ |
|---|---|
| Prime cost (300 + 400) | 700 |
| Production overheads (50 × \$26) | 1,300 |
| Total production cost | 2,000 |
| Non-production overheads (1.20 × 700) | 840 |
| Total cost | 2,840 |

**185 B**

Finished output = (20,000 + 110,000 – 40,000) = 90,000 units.

Closing WIP = 40,000 units 50% complete = 20,000 equivalent units.

Cost per equivalent unit (in \$000) = \$132,000/(90,000 + 20,000)

= \$1,200 per equivalent unit/finished car.

**186 B**

The total value of WIP will increase. The number of equivalent units will increase which will cause the cost per unit to decrease.

**187 C**

Normal loss is 10% of input = 20 kg.

Actual loss = 50 kg

Abnormal loss = 50 – 20 = 30 kg

Equivalent units of output:

| | *Total* | *Materials* | *Conversion* |
|---|---|---|---|
| Finished output | 150 | 150 | 150 |
| Abnormal loss | 30 | 30 | 15 |
| Total EUs | 180 | 180 | 165 |

Cost per equivalent unit:

Material cost = 200 × $ 4 = $800
Labour and overheads cost = 100× $ 15 + $1,000 = $2,500

Materials = $800/180 = $4.44
Conversion = $2,500/165 = $15.15

Total cost of completed unit = $(4.44 + 15.15) = $19.59

**188 A**

**Process account**

| | **Units** | | **Units** |
|---|---|---|---|
| Opening WIP | 2,000 | Finished | 11,000 |
| Started | 12,000 | Closing WIP | 3,000 |
| | 14,000 | | 14,000 |

| | | |
|---|---|---|
| Units started and finished = 11,000 – 2,000 | = | 9,000 |
| Closing WIP = 3,000 x 20% | = | 600 |
| Opening WIP = 2,000 x 30% | = | 600 |
| | | **10,200** |

**189 C**

Cost per unit = (1,200 + 3,500 – 30) / 200 – 30 = 27.47 per kg

27.47 × 190 = $5,219

**190 A**

Process costing is used for companies producing large quantities of similar products (homogeneous output) and these are valued at average cost.

**191 A**

| | $ |
|---|---|
| Direct materials 120 kg @ $4 per kg | 480 |
| Direct labour: 3 hours @ $10 per hour | 30 |
| 20 hours @ $5 per hour | 100 |
| Hire of machine: 2 days @ $100 per day | 200 |
| Overhead 23 hours @ $8 per hour | 184 |
| | 994 |
| Price charged | 942 |
| Loss | (52) |

# SERVICE AND OPERATION COSTING

**192 C**

A service industry is an industry not involved in agriculture, mining, construction or manufacturing. Transport industries are service industries.

**193 C**

Services are usually (but not always) associated with labour and labour costs, low material costs and relatively high indirect costs. Service costing also makes use of composite cost units, such as the cost per guest/day, cost per patient/day, cost per passenger/mile and so on.

**194 D**

A charitable foundation will be a not-for-profit organisation.

**195 B**

Average cost per occupied bed per day

$$= \frac{\text{Total cost}}{\text{Number of beds occupied}}$$

$$= \frac{\$100{,}000 + \$5{,}000 + \$22{,}500}{6{,}450 \times 2} = \$9.88$$

or 127,500/(200 × 2 + 30) × 30 = $9.88

**196 A**

Contribution = sales revenue – variable costs

= $(7,000 – 780 – 400 – 200) = $5,620

**197 A**

Breakeven point = ($3,600,000 + $1,500,000)/$5,620 = 907.47 treatments, say 907

Margin of safety = 950 – 907 = 43

**198 B**

| | $ | $ |
|---|---|---|
| Cost per: | | |
| Millions of units sold | 208 | 104 |
| Thousand consumers | 750 | 625 |
| $m of sales | 33,333 | 20,000 |

The cost per unit sold, per consumer and per $m of sales are all higher for Company A than for Company B indicating that Company A is less efficient than Company B.

**199 B**

$$\text{Room occupancy \%} = \frac{\text{Total number of rooms occupied daily}}{\text{Rooms available to be let}} \times 100\%$$

$$= \frac{200 + 30}{240 + 40} \times 100\% = 82.1\%$$

**200 C**

A service is intangible and inventory cannot be held. Services generally have a high level of fixed costs and there are often difficulties in identifying a suitable cost unit.

# BUDGETING

**201 B**

The main purposes of budgeting are to plan and control. Budgets also usually give authority to spend up to the budget limit. Budgets are not primarily used for decision making.

**202 B**

False is the correct answer because the budget committee is made up from senior managers of each function in the organisation.

**203 B**

**Selling price and cost structure**

If C/S ratio = 75%, variable costs are 25% of selling price.

Therefore, selling price = $50/0.25 = $200.

| | *Current year* *$/unit* | *Next year* *$/unit* |
|---|---|---|
| Selling price | 200 | 216 |
| Less: Variable cost | (50) | (56) |
| Contribution | 150 | 160 |
| Total fixed costs ($70 × 5,000) | $350,000 | $392,000 |
| Profit | $400,000 | $400,000 |

Minimum number of units to achieve a required profit of $400,000

= $(400,000 + 392,000) ÷ $160

= 4,950

**204 B**

| | |
|---|---|
| Units required | 100,000 |
| Less: opening inventory | (14,000) |
| Add: closing inventory required (14,000 × 0.6) | 8,400 |
| | 94,400 |

**205 B**

False is the correct answer because the production budget is the sales budget **plus** closing inventory of finished goods **minus** opening inventory of finished goods.

**206 B**

4,500/0.9 = 5,000 litres.

Note that opening and closing inventories are relevant to the material purchases budget, not the material usage budget.

**207 A**

True is the correct answer because the material usage budget is the material requirement for the units produced.

**208 C**

| | | $ |
|---|---|---|
| Product A | 1,750 units × 3 hours/unit × $7 /hour | 36,750 |
| Product B | 5,000 units × 4 hours/unit × $7 /hour | 140,000 |
| | | 176,750 |

**209 B**

False is the correct answer because the volume variance is the difference between the fixed and flexible budget.

**210 B**

Flexed budget:

| | *Budget* | *Flexed Budget* | *Actual* |
|---|---|---|---|
| Sales (units) | 120,000 | 100,000 | 100,000 |
| | $000 | $000 | $000 |
| Sales revenue | 1,200 | 1,000 | 995 |
| Variable printing costs | 360 | 300 | 280 |
| Variable production overheads | 60 | 50 | 56 |
| Fixed production cost | 300 | 300 | 290 |
| Fixed administration cost | 360 | 360 | 364 |
| Profit/(Loss) | 120 | (10) | 5 |

**211 A**

The expenditure variance is measured by the difference between the flexed budget and the actual cost.

The expenditure variance is $15,000 favourable.

The volume variance is measured by the difference between the original budget and the flexed budget.

The volume variance is $130,000 adverse.

**212 D**

A principal budget factor is defined as the factor acting as the constraint on the overall level of activity in a period. It is often sales demand, but could be a key production resource or cash.

**213 D**

If 1X and 2Y are sold, this earns $250. Call this a batch.

The company wants to earn $100,000.

$100,000 / 250 = 400 batches.

This is 400 X and 800 Y

**214 D**

A budget manual will include all of the options.

**215 B**

| | *Units* |
|---|---|
| Budgeted sales | 2,300 |
| Current inventory | (400) |
| Closing inventory required | 550 |
| Production | 2,450 |

**216 A**

Machine hours required:

| | |
|---|---|
| X | 1,000 hours |
| Y | 2,400 hours |
| Z | 600 hours |
| Total | 4,000 |

Overhead budget:

Variable: 4,000 × $2.30 = $9,200

Fixed: 4,000 × $0.75 = $3,000

Total = $(9,200 +3,000) = $12,200

**217 C**

| | *Clockwork clown* | *Wind-up train* | *Total* |
|---|---|---|---|
| Budgeted sales | 450 | 550 | |
| + Closing inventory | 30 | 40 | |
| – Opening inventory | (20) | (50) | |
| Production budget | 460 | 540 | |
| Material usage | × 2 kg | × 1 kg | |
| Material usage budget | 920 kg | 540 kg | 1,460 kg |

**218 A**

| | |
|---|---|
| Total material usage | 1,460 kg |
| + Closing inventory | 60 |
| – Opening inventory | (50) |
| Total material purchases | 1,470 kg |
| Material purchases budget = 1,470 × $5 | $7,350 |

**219 A**

| | *Clockwork clown* | *Wind-up train* |
|---|---|---|
| Budgeted sales | 450 | 550 |
| + Closing inventory | 30 | 40 |
| – Opening inventory | (20) | (50) |
| Production budget | 460 | 540 |
| Labour | × 18/60 | × 30/60 |
| | 138 hours | 270 hours |
| Total | 408 hours × $8 = $3,264 | |

**220 D**

Paid hours including idle time = 2,400 × 100/80 = 3,000

Budgeted labour cost = 3,000 hours × $10 = $30,000

## STANDARD COSTING

**221 D**

All the techniques listed in the question could be used to monitor and control costs.

**222 C**

The standard labour rate should be the expected rate/hour, but allowing for standard levels of idle time. For example, if the work force is paid $9 per hour but idle time of 10% is expected, the standard labour rate will be $10 per hour, not $9.

**223 D**

| | |
|---|---|
| Standard contribution on actual sales | $10,000 |
| Add : favourable sales price variance | $500 |
| Less : Adverse total variable costs variance | $(2,000) |
| **Actual Contribution** | **$8,500** |

The standard contribution on actual sales has been obtained by adjusting the budgeted contribution by the sales volume contribution variance. Therefore, this variance should have been ignored in answering the question.

**224 A**

| | |
|---|---|
| Sales contribution on actual sales | $50,000 |
| Less adverse total variable costs variance | $3,500 |
| Actual contribution | $46,500 |

No adjustment is required for the favourable sales volume contribution variance : it would have already been added to the budgeted contribution to arrive at the satndard contribution from actual sales given in the question. The total fixed costs variance, along with budgeted fixed costs, appears in a reconciliation statement below the actual contribution.

**225 D**

| | $ | |
|---|---|---|
| 14,000 hours should cost (× $10) | 140,000 | |
| They did cost | 176,000 | |
| Labour rate variance | 36,000 | (A) |
| | *Hours* | |
| 5,500 units should take (× 3 hours) | 16,500 | |
| They did take | 14,000 | |
| Labour efficiency variance in hours | 2,500 | (F) |
| × labour rate | $10 | |
| Labour efficiency variance in $ | $25,000 | (F) |

**226 D**

Expenditure variance:

Monthly budgeted production (10,800/12) = 900 units

| *Monthly budgeted expenditure (Flexed budget)* | $ | |
|---|---|---|
| Fixed costs (900 × $4) | 3,600 | |
| Variable costs (800 × $6) | 4,800 | |
| Total expected expenditure | 8,400 | |
| Actual expenditure | 8,500 | |
| Expenditure variance | 100 | (A) |

Volume variance:

This only applies to fixed overhead costs:

| | |
|---|---|
| Volume variance in units (900 – 800) | 100 units (A) |
| Standard fixed overhead cost per unit | $4 |
| Fixed overhead volume variance | $400 (A) |

**227 C**

| | $ | |
|---|---|---|
| Expenditure variance (= 10% of budgeted expenditure) | 36,000 | (A) |
| Therefore budgeted expenditure | 360,000 | |
| Actual expenditure | 396,000 | |

**228 C**

Fixed production overhead cost per unit = $120,000/20,000 units = $6 per unit.

| | *Units* | |
|---|---|---|
| Budgeted output | 20,000 | |
| Actual output | 21,000 | |
| Volume variance in units | 1,000 | (F) |
| Fixed overhead cost per unit | $6 | |
| Fixed overhead volume variance | $6,000 | (F) |

**229 A**

Budgeted hours of work = 30,000 units × 4 hours = 120,000 hours.

Fixed overhead absorption rate/hour = $840,000/120,000 hours = $7/hour.

| | *hours* | |
|---|---|---|
| Budgeted hours of work | 120,000 | |
| Actual hours of work | 123,000 | |
| Capacity variance in hours | 3,000 | favourable |
| Standard fixed overhead rate/hour | $7 | |
| Fixed overhead capacity variance in $ | **$21,000 favourable** | |

**230 C**

Budgeted fixed overhead cost per unit = $48,000/4,800 units = $10.

| | $ | |
|---|---|---|
| Budgeted fixed overhead | 48,000 | |
| Expenditure variance | 2,000 | (A) |
| Actual fixed overhead | 50,000 | |

| | $ |
|---|---|
| Actual fixed overhead | 50,000 |
| Under-absorbed fixed overhead | 8,000 |
| Absorbed overhead | 42,000 |

Units produced = Absorbed overhead/Absorption rate per unit

= $42,000/$10 = 4,200 units.

**231 C**

This is a definition of 'basic standards'. Basic standards are not widely used in practice.

**232 A**

True is the correct answer because quality is of increasing importance. This means that materials are often bought on long-term contracts and a premium may be paid for quality. Staff may be multi-skilled and more experienced and therefore paid a higher wage rate. Management may be more concerned about the quality of the process than achieving standard costs.

**233 C**

Less experienced staff are likely to be paid at a lower rate and therefore the labour rate variance will be favourable.

Usage of materials is likely to be unfavourable as the staff are less experienced, thus there will be more wastage and a higher level of rejects.

**234 D**

Usage of materials is likely to be unfavourable as the materials are sub-standard, thus there will be more wastage and a higher level of rejects.

Time spent by the labour force on rejected items that will not become output leads to higher than standard time spent per unit of output.

**235 A**

| | | |
|---|---|---|
| Actual labour cost | = | \$(116,000 – 5,800) |
| | = | \$110,200 |
| Actual labour hours | = | $30{,}000 - \frac{\$4{,}000}{\$4}$ |
| | = | 29,000 |
| Actual rate per hour | = | $\frac{\$110{,}200}{29{,}000}$ |
| | = | \$3.80 |

**236 D**

| | |
|---|---|
| Rate variance | = Actual hours × Standard rate – Actual labour cost |
| – \$706 | = 10,080 × Standard rate – \$8,770 |
| Standard rate | = $\frac{\$(8{,}770 - 706)}{10{,}080}$ |
| | = \$0.80 per hour |
| Efficiency variance | = (Standard hours – Actual hours) × Standard rate |
| \$256 | = (Standard time per unit × 5,000 – 10,080) × \$0.80 |

Standard time per unit $= \dfrac{(\$256 \div \$0.80) + 10{,}080}{5{,}000}$

= 2.08 hours

**Alternatively:**

| | $ | |
|---|---|---|
| Actual hours paid @ actual rate (worked) | | |
| $10{,}080 \times \dfrac{\$8{,}770}{10{,}080}$ | 8,770 | |
| | | $706 A |
| Actual hours paid @ standard rate (worked) | | |
| $10{,}080 \times (\dfrac{\$8{,}064}{10{,}080})$ | ∴ 8,064 | |
| | | $256 F |
| Standard hours @ standard rate | | |
| $5{,}000 \times ? \times \dfrac{\$8{,}064}{10{,}080}$ | ∴ 8,320 | |

$5{,}000 \times ? \times \dfrac{\$8{,}064}{10{,}080}$ = $8,320

? = $2.08

**237 C**

| | |
|---|---|
| 710 units should take | 355 hours |
| Did take (378 – 20) | 358 hours |
| | 3 hours adverse |
| × $12 | $36 adverse |

**238 C**

Expenditure variance = (actual quantity × actual price) – (actual quantity × standard price)

= $7,700 – (4,800× $1.5) = $500 adverse

Efficiency variance = (actual quantity × standard price) – (standard quantity × standard price)

= (4,800 × $1.5) – (500 × 10 × $1.50) = $300 favourable

**239 B**

(Budgeted quantity – Actual quantity) × standard profit per unit

(1,000 – 900) × ($50 – $39) = $1,100

**240 A**

| | |
|---|---|
| Budgeted overhead – actual overhead | = $1,250 |
| Actual overhead | = 0.98 × Budgeted overhead |
| Budgeted overhead – (0.98 × Budgeted overhead) | = $1,250 |
| Budgeted overhead | = $1,250 ÷ 0.02 = $62,500 |
| Actual overhead | = $(62,500 – 1,250) = $61,250 |

**241 C**

**242 B**

This statement is false because the sales volume variance under marginal costing is based on standard contribution per unit (whereas the sales volume variance under absorption costing is based on standard profit per unit).

**243 D**

[(45,600 kg × $4) – $173,280] = $9,120 favourable

**244 A**

| | $ |
|---|---|
| Actual usage at standard cost (45,600 × $4) | 182,400 |
| Less: Adverse usage variance | (15,200) |
| Standard cost for actual production | 167,200 |
| Actual production (units) = ($167,200 ÷ $50) = | 3,344 |

**245 B**

The purchase of the new machine is likely to result in improved efficiency but higher depreciation costs.

**246 D**

(3700 – 4,000) x 1.5 x $2.40 = $1,080 (A)

**247 C**

(i) will affect the sales price variance.

**248 D**

Standard price of materials = $76,500/1,500 kg = $51/kg.

Standard materials usage = 1,500 kg/600 = 2.5 kg per unit.

| | *kg* | |
|---|---|---|
| 580 units should use (× 2.5) | 1,450 | |
| Did use | 1,566 | |
| Usage variance in kg | 116 | (A) |
| Standard price per kg | $51 | |
| Usage variance in kg | $5,916 | (A) |

**249 D**

Usage variance = $300 (A)

Usage variance in kg = $300 (A)/$2 per kg = 150 kg (A)

| | *Kg* | |
|---|---|---|
| 500 units should use (× 3) | 1,500 | |
| Usage variance in kg | 150 | (A) |
| 500 units did use | 1,650 | |
| Increase in inventory (400 – 100) | 300 | |
| Material purchases in kg | 1,950 | |

**250 A**

Standard price per kg = $25,500/1,500 kg = $17

| | $ | |
|---|---|---|
| 1,566 kg should cost (× $17) | 26,622 | |
| Did cost | 25,839 | |
| Material P price variance | 783 | (F) |

**251 C**

| | $ |
|---|---|
| Actual cost | 144,500 |
| Standard cost of actual production (8,500 × $15) | 127,500 |
| Total fixed overhead variance | 17,000 adverse |

**252 A**

The standard contribution per unit is $(50 – 4 – 16 – 10 – 1) = $19.

| | | |
|---|---|---|
| Budgeted sales volume | 3,000 | units |
| Actual sales volume | 3,500 | units |
| Sales volume variance in units | 500 | units (F) |

| | |
|---|---|
| Standard contribution per unit | $19 |
| Sales volume variance in $ | $9,500 (F) |

**253 C**

| | *Units* | |
|---|---|---|
| Budgeted sales units | 10,000 | |
| Actual sales units | 9,800 | |
| Sales volume variance (units) | 200 | (A) |
| Standard profit/unit | $5 | |
| Sales volume profit variance ($) | $1,000 | (A) |

**254 B**

Capacity variance (5,000 – 5,500) hours at $15 per hour = 7,500 (F)

**255 B**

| | $ | |
|---|---|---|
| Actual labour cost | 117,600 | |
| Rate variance | 8,400 | (A) |
| Standard cost of hours worked | 109,200 | |

| | |
|---|---|
| Hours worked | 28,000 |
| Standard rate per hour ($109,200/28,000 hours) | $3.90 |

Efficiency variance in hours = $3,900 (F)/$3.90 per hour = 1,000 hours (F)

| | *Hours* | |
|---|---|---|
| Actual hours worked | 28,000 | |
| Efficiency variance in hours | 1,000 | (F) |
| Standard hours for actual production | 29,000 | |

# APPENDIX: SPREADSHEETS

**256 C**

A database contains records and files and is most suitable for storing large volumes of data

**257 C**

The formula for correlation is $r = \dfrac{n\sum xy - (\sum x)(\sum y)}{\sqrt{\{n\sum x^2 - (\sum x)^2\}\{n\sum y^2 - (\sum y)^2\}}}$

Here n is 7 and to construct the formula we need to identify the appropriate totals from row 11.

A and D are wrong because they use n = 6.

B is wrong because it lacks the square root required for the bottom of the formula.

**258 B**

All are said to be advantages of spreadsheet software with the exception of (i) security. A computer-based approach exposes the firm to threats from viruses, hackers and general system failure.

**259 D**

Budgeted production for a period = budgeted sales for the period + closing inventory of finished goods for the period –opening inventory of finished goods for the period.

Here
F3 + 10% of F4 – 10% of F3 = budgeted production for March

**260 B**

Using graphics is usually done using the chart wizard not the format cells option.

# Section 3

# PILOT PAPER EXAM QUESTIONS

1 **The following break-even chart has been drawn showing lines for total cost (TC), total variable cost (TVC), total fixed cost (TFC) and total sales revenue (TSR):**

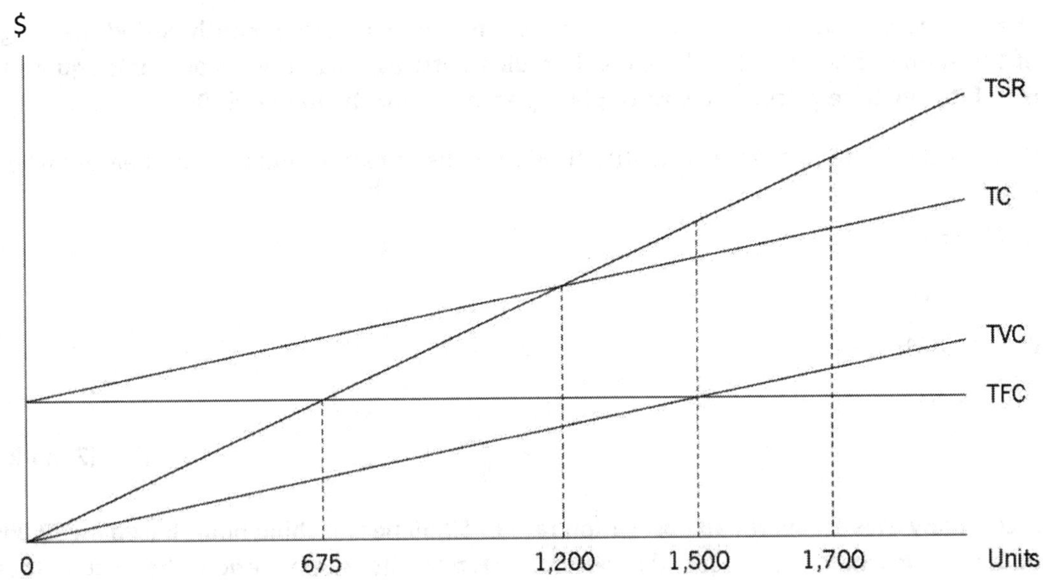


What is the margin of safety at the 1,700 units level of activity?

A 200 units

B 300 units

C 500 units

D 1,025 units **(2 marks)**

2 **The following assertions relate to financial accounting and to cost accounting:**

(i) The main users of financial accounting information are external to an organisation.

(ii) Cost accounting is that part of financial accounting which records the cash received and payments made by an organisation.

Which of the following statements are true?

A Assertions (i) and (ii) are both correct

B Only assertion (i) is correct

C Only assertion (ii) is correct

**(1 mark)**

**3** **Regression analysis is being used to find the line of best fit (y = a + bx) from eleven pairs of data. The calculations have produced the following information:**

Σx = 440, Σy = 330, Σx2 = 17,986, Σy2 = 10,366, Σxy = 13,467 and b = 0.69171

What is the value of 'a' in the equation for the line of best fit (to 2 decimal places)?

A 0.63

B 0.69

C 2.33

D 5.33

**(2 marks)**

**4** **The purchase price of a stock item is $25 per unit. In each three month period the usage of the item is 20,000 units. The annual holding costs associated with one unit equate to 6% of its purchase price. The cost of placing an order for the item is $20.**

What is the Economic Order Quantity (EOQ) for the inventory item to the nearest whole unit?

A 730

B 894

C 1,461

D 1,633

**(2 marks)**

**5** **A company uses an overhead absorption rate of $3.50 per machine hour, based on 32,000 budgeted machine hours for the period. During the same period the actual total overhead expenditure amounted to $108,875 and 30,000 machine hours were recorded on actual production.**

By how much was the total overhead under or over absorbed for the period?

A Under absorbed by $3,875

B Under absorbed by $7,000

C Over absorbed by $3,875

D Over absorbed by $7,000

**(2 marks)**

**6** **For which of the following is a profit centre manager responsible?**

A Costs only

B Revenues only

C Costs and revenues

**(1 mark)**

**7 An organisation has the following total costs at two activity levels:**

| | | |
|---|---|---|
| Activity level (units) | 16,000 | 22,000 |
| Total costs ($) | 135,000 | 170,000 |

Variable cost per unit is constant within this range of activity but there is a step up of $5,000 in the total fixed costs when the activity exceeds 17,500 units.

What is the total cost at an activity of 20,000 units?

A $155,000

B $158,000

C $160,000

D $163,000

**(2 marks)**

**8 A company manufactures and sells a single product. In two consecutive months the following levels of production and sales (in units) occurred:**

| | *Month 1* | *Month 2* |
|---|---|---|
| Sales | 3,800 | 4,400 |
| Production | 3,900 | 4,200 |

The opening inventory for Month 1 was 400 units. Profits or losses have been calculated for each month using both absorption and marginal costing principles.

Which of the following combination of profits and losses for the two months is consistent with the above data?

| | *Absorption costing profit/(loss)* | | *Marginal costing profit/(loss)* | |
|---|---|---|---|---|
| | *Month 1* | *Month 2* | *Month 1* | *Month 2* |
| A | 200 | 4,400 | (400) | 3,200 |
| B | (400) | 4,400 | 200 | 3,200 |
| C | 200 | 3,200 | (400) | 4,400 |
| D | (400) | 3,200 | 200 | 4,400 |

**(2 marks)**

**9 Which of the following best describes a flexible budget?**

A A budget which shows variable production costs only

B A monthly budget which is changed to reflect the number of days in the month

C A budget which shows sales revenue and costs at different levels of activity

D A budget that is updated halfway through the year to incorporate the actual results for the first half of the year

**(2 marks)**

**10 Information relating to two processes (F and G) was as follows:**

| Process | *Normal loss as % of input* | *Input litres* | *Output litres* |
|---|---|---|---|
| F | 8 | 65,000 | 58,900 |
| G | 5 | 37,500 | 35,700 |

For each process, was there an abnormal loss or an abnormal gain?

| | *Process F* | *Process G* |
|---|---|---|
| A | Abnormal gain | Abnormal gain |
| B | Abnormal gain | Abnormal loss |
| C | Abnormal loss | Abnormal gain |
| D | Abnormal loss | Abnormal loss |

**(2 marks)**

**11 An organisation manufactures a single product which is sold for $80 per unit. The organisation's total monthly fixed costs are $99,000 and it has a contribution to sales ratio of 45%. This month it plans to manufacture and sell 4,000 units.**

What is the organisation's margin of safety this month (in units)?

A 1,250

B 1,750

C 2,250

D 2,750

**(2 marks)**

**12 Which one of the following should be classified as indirect labour?**

A Assembly workers on a car production line

B Bricklayers in a house building company

C Machinists in a factory producing clothes

D Forklift truck drivers in the stores of an engineering company

**(2 marks)**

**13 A company is evaluating a project that requires 400kg of raw material X. The company has 150kg of X in inventory that were purchased six months ago for $55 per kg. The company no longer has any use for X. The inventory of X could be sold for $40 per kg. The current purchase price for X is $53 per kg.**

What is the total relevant cost of raw material X for the project?

A $17,950

B $19,250

C $21,200

D $21,500

**(2 marks)**

**14 Which of the following is NOT a feasible value for the correlation coefficient?**

A +1.4

B +0.7

C 0

D −0.7

**(2 marks)**

**15 The following statements relate to aspects of budget administration:**

Statement (1): An important task of a budget committee is to ensure that budgets are properly coordinated.

Statement (2): A budget manual is the document produced at the end of the budget setting process.

Which of the following is true?

A Only statement (1) is correct

B Only statement (2) is correct

C Both statements are correct

**(1 mark)**

**16 Up to a given level of activity in each period the purchase price per unit of a raw material is constant. After that point a lower price per unit applies both to further units purchased and also retrospectively to all units already purchased.**

Which of the following graphs depicts the total cost of the raw materials for a period?

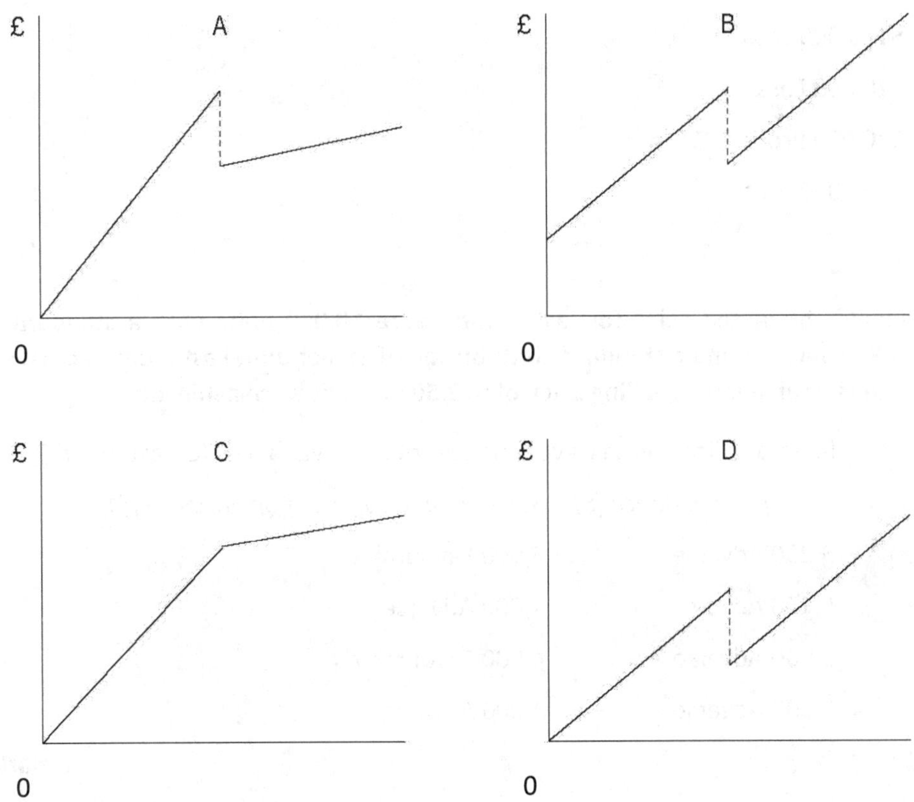


**(2 marks)**

**17 A manufacturing organisation incurs costs relating to the following:**

(1) Commission payable to salespersons.

(2) Inspecting all products.

(3) Packing the products at the end of the manufacturing process prior to moving them to the warehouse.

Which of these costs are classified as production costs?

A (1) and (2) only

B (1) and (3) only

C (2) and (3) only

D (1), (2) and (3)

**(2 marks)**

**18 Which of the following is correct with regard to expected values?**

A Expected values provide a weighted average of anticipated outcomes

B The expected value will always equal one of the possible outcomes

C Expected values will show the decision maker's attitude to risk

D The expected value will never equal one of the possible outcomes

**(2 marks)**

**19 There is a 60% chance that a company will make a profit of $300,000 next year and a 40% chance of making a loss of $400,000.**

What is the expected profit or loss for next year?

A $120,000 Loss

B $20,000 Loss

C $20,000 Profit

D $120,000 Profit

**(2 marks)**

**20 A company's budgeted sales for last month were 10,000 units with a standard selling price of $20 per unit and a standard contribution of $8 per unit. Last month actual sales of 10,500 units at an average selling price of $19.50 per unit were achieved.**

What were the sales price and sales volume contribution variances for last month?

| | *Sales price variance ($)* | *Sales volume contribution variance ($)* |
|---|---|---|
| A | 5,250 Adverse | 4,000 Favourable |
| B | 5,250 Adverse | 4,000 Adverse |
| C | 5,000 Adverse | 4,000 Favourable |
| D | 5,000 Adverse | 4,000 Adverse |

**(2 marks)**

**21 A company manufactures and sells one product which requires 8 kg of raw material in its manufacture. The budgeted data relating to the next period are as follows:**

| | Units |
|---|---|
| Sales | 19,000 |
| Opening inventory of finished goods | 4,000 |
| Closing inventory of finished goods | 3,000 |
| | Kg |
| Opening inventory of raw materials | 50,000 |
| Closing inventory of raw materials | 53,000 |

What is the budgeted raw material purchases for next period (in kg)?

A 141,000

B 147,000

C 157,000

D 163,000

**(2 marks)**

**22 The following statements refer to spreadsheets:**

(i) A spreadsheet is the most suitable software for the storage of large volumes of data.

(ii) A spreadsheet could be used to produce a flexible budget.

(iii) Most spreadsheets contain a facility to display the data within them in a graphical form.

Which of these statements are correct?

A (i) and (ii) only

B (i) and (iii) only

C (ii) and (iii) only

D (i), (ii) and (iii)

**(2 marks)**

**23 A company always determines its order quantity for a raw material by using the Economic Order Quantity (EOQ) model.**

What would be the effects on the EOQ and the total annual holding cost of a decrease in the cost of ordering a batch of raw material?

| | *EOQ* | *Annual holding cost* |
|---|---|---|
| A | Higher | Lower |
| B | Higher | Higher |
| C | Lower | Higher |
| D | Lower | Lower |

**(2 marks)**

**24 Which one of the following is most likely to operate a system of service costing?**

A A printing company

B A hospital

C A firm of solicitors **(1 mark)**

**25 The following budgeted information relates to a manufacturing company for next period:**

| | Units | | $ |
|---|---|---|---|
| Production | 14,000 | Fixed production costs | 63,000 |
| Sales | 12,000 | Fixed selling costs | 12,000 |

The normal level of activity is 14,000 units per period.

Using absorption costing the profit for next period has been calculated as $36,000.

What would the profit for next period be using marginal costing?

A $25,000

B $27,000

C $45,000

D $47,000 **(2 marks)**

**26 A company manufactures a single product which it sells for $20 per unit. The product has a contribution to sales ratio of 40%. The company's weekly breakeven point is sales revenue of $18,000.**

What would be the profit in a week when 1,200 units are sold?

A $1,200

B $2,400

C $3,600

D $6,000 **(2 marks)**

**27 The following graph relates to a linear programming problem:**

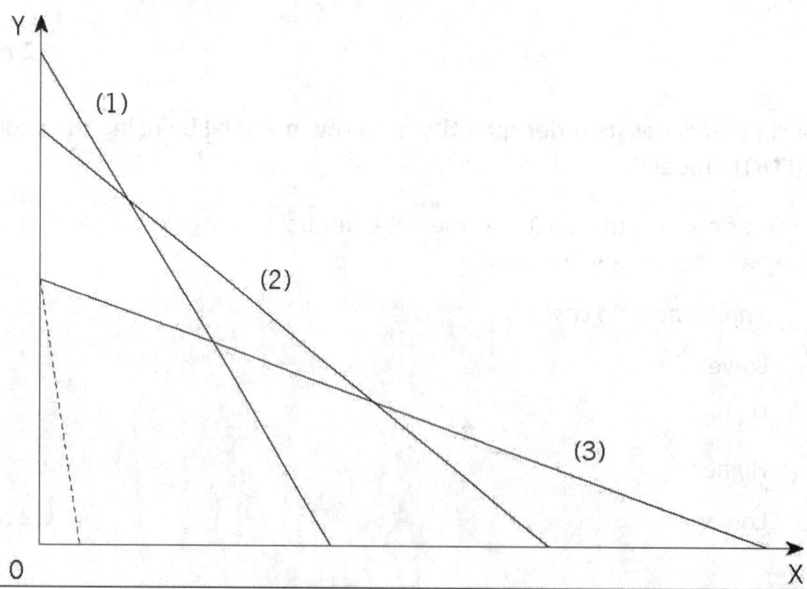

The objective is to maximise contribution and the dotted line on the graph depicts this function. There are three constraints which are all of the 'less than or equal to' type which are depicted on the graph by the three solid lines labelled (1), (2) and (3).

At which of the following intersections is contribution maximised?

A Constraints (1) and (2)

B Constraints (2) and (3)

C Constraints (1) and (3)

D Constraint (1) and the x-axis

**(2 marks)**

**28 In an organisation manufacturing a number of different products in one large factory, the rent of that factory is an example of a direct expense when costing a product.**

Is this statement true or false?

A True

B False **(1 mark)**

**29 A company operates a process in which no losses are incurred. The process account for last month, when there was no opening work-in-progress, was as follows:**

| | $ | | $ |
|---|---|---|---|
| Costs arising | 624,000 | Finished output (10,000 units) | 480,000 |
| | | Closing work-in-progress (4,000 units) | 144,000 |
| | 624,000 | | 624,000 |

The closing work-in-progress was complete to the same degree for all elements of cost.

What was the percentage degree of completion of the closing work-in-progress?

A 12%

B 30%

C 40%

D 75% **(2 marks)**

**30 A company manufactures and sells two products (X and Y) both of which utilise the same skilled labour. For the coming period, the supply of skilled labour is limited to 2,000 hours.**

Data relating to each product are as follows:

| Product | X | Y |
|---|---|---|
| Selling price per unit | $20 | $40 |
| Variable cost per unit | $12 | $30 |
| Skilled labour hours per unit | 2 | 4 |
| Maximum demand (units) per period | 800 | 400 |

In order to maximise profit in the coming period, how many units of each product should the company manufacture and sell?

A 200 units of X and 400 units of Y

B 400 units of X and 300 units of Y

C 600 units of X and 200 units of Y

D 800 units of X and 100 units of Y

**(2 marks)**

**31 The following statements refer to organisations using job costing:**

(i) Work is done to customer specification.

(ii) Work is usually completed within a relatively short period of time.

(iii) Products manufactured tend to be all identical.

Which two of these statements are CORRECT?

A (i) and (ii)

B (i) and (iii)

C (ii) and (iii)

**(1 mark)**

---

**The following information relates to questions 32 and 33:**

A company uses standard costing and the standard variable overhead cost for a product is:

6 direct labour hours @ $10 per hour

Last month when 3,900 units of the product were manufactured, the actual expenditure on variable overheads was $235,000 and 24,000 hours were actually worked.

---

**32 What was the variable overhead expenditure variance for last month?**

A $5,000 Adverse

B $5,000 Favourable

C $6,000 Adverse

D $6,000 Favourable

**(2 marks)**

**33 What was the variable overhead efficiency variance for last month?**

A $5,000 Adverse

B $5,000 Favourable

C $6,000 Adverse

D $6,000 Favourable

**(2 marks)**

**34** **When a manufacturing company operates a standard marginal costing system there are no fixed production overhead variances.**

Is this statement true or false?

A True

B False

**(1 mark)**

**35** **A company operates a standard costing system. The variance analysis for last month shows a favourable materials price variance and an adverse labour efficiency variance.**

The following four statements, which make comparisons with the standards, have been made:

(1) Inferior quality materials were purchased and used.

(2) Superior quality materials were purchased and used.

(3) Lower graded workers were used on production.

(4) Higher graded workers were used on production.

Which statements are consistent with the variance analysis?

A (1) and (3)

B (1) and (4)

C (2) and (3)

D (2) and (4) **(2 marks)**

**36** **Which of the following best describes a principal budget factor?**

A A factor that affects all budget centres.

B A factor that is controllable by a budget centre manager.

C A factor which limits the activities of an organisation.

D A factor that the management accountant builds into all budgets. **(2 marks)**

**37** **Four vertical lines have been labelled G, H, J and K at different levels of activity on the following profit-volume chart:**

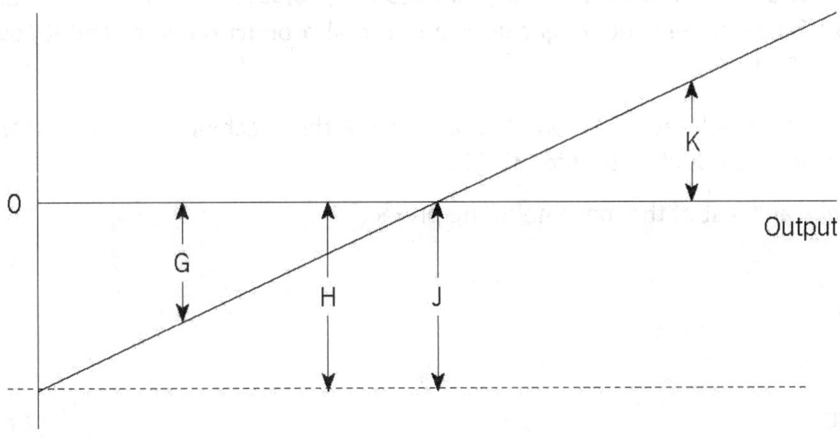

Which line represents the total contribution at that level of activity?

A Line G

B Line H

C Line J

D Line K **(2 marks)**

**38 Data is information that has been processed in such a way as to be meaningful to its recipients.**

Is this statement true or false?

A True

B False **(1 mark)**

**39 Two products G and H are created from a joint process. G can be sold immediately after split-off. H requires further processing into product HH before it is in a saleable condition. There are no opening inventories and no work-in-progress of products G, H or HH. The following data are available for last period:**

| | | $ |
|---|---|---|
| Total joint production costs | | 350,000 |
| Further processing costs of product H | | 66,000 |
| *Product* | *Production units* | *Closing inventory units* |
| G | 420,000 | 20,000 |
| HH | 330,000 | 30,000 |

Using the physical unit method for apportioning joint production costs, what was the cost value of the closing inventory of product HH for last period?

A $16,640

B $18,625

C $20,000

D $21,600

**(2 marks)**

**40 A company purchased a machine several years ago for $50,000. Its written down value is now $10,000. The machine is no longer used on normal production work and it could be sold now for $8,000.**

A project is being considered which would make use of this machine for six months. After this time the machine would be sold for $5,000.

What is the relevant cost of the machine to the project?

A $2,000

B $3,000

C $5,000

D $10,000 **(2 marks)**

**41 A company operates a standard absorption costing system. The standard fixed production overhead rate is $15 per hour.**

The following data relate to last month:

| | |
|---|---|
| Actual hours worked | 5,500 |
| Budgeted hours | 5,000 |
| Standard hours for actual production | 4,800 |

What was the fixed production overhead capacity variance?

A $7,500 Adverse

B $7,500 Favourable

C $10,500 Adverse

D $10,500 Favourable

**(2 marks)**

**42 The following statements relate to relevant cost concepts in decision-making:**

(i) Materials can never have an opportunity cost whereas labour can.

(ii) The annual depreciation charge is not a relevant cost.

(iii) Fixed costs would have a relevant cost element if a decision causes a change in their total expenditure.

Which statements are correct?

A (i) and (ii) only

B (i) and (iii) only

C (ii) and (iii) only

D (i), (ii) and (iii)

**(2 marks)**

**43 A contract is under consideration which requires 600 labour hours to complete. There are 350 hours of spare labour capacity for which the workers are still being paid the normal rate of pay. The remaining hours for the contract can be found either by weekend overtime working paid at double the normal rate of pay or by diverting labour from other production. This other production makes a contribution, net of labour cost, of $5 per hour. The normal rate of pay is $9 per hour.**

What is the total relevant cost of labour for the contract?

A $1,250

B $3,500

C $4,500

D $4,900

**(2 marks)**

**44 An organisation operates a piecework system of remuneration, but also guarantees its employees 80% of a time-based rate of pay which is based on $20 per hour for an eight hour working day. Three minutes is the standard time allowed per unit of output. Piecework is paid at the rate of $18 per standard hour.**

If an employee produces 200 units in eight hours on a particular day, what is the employee's gross pay for that day?

A $128

B $144

C $160

D $180

**(2 marks)**

**45 A semi-variable cost is one that, in the short term, remains the same over a given range of activity but beyond that increases and then remains constant at the higher level of activity.**

Is this statement true or false?

A True

B False

**(1 mark)**

**46 A factory consists of two production cost centres (P and Q) and two service cost centres (X and Y). The total allocated and apportioned overhead for each is as follows:**

| P | Q | X | Y |
|---|---|---|---|
| $95,000 | $82,000 | $46,000 | $30,000 |

It has been estimated that each service cost centre does work for other cost centres in the following proportions:

| | *P* | *Q* | *X* | *Y* |
|---|---|---|---|---|
| Percentage of service cost centre X to | 50 | 50 | – | – |
| Percentage of service cost centre Y to | 30 | 60 | 10 | – |

The reapportionment of service cost centre costs to other cost centres fully reflects the above proportions.

After the reapportionment of service cost centre costs has been carried out, what is the total overhead for production cost centre P?

A $124,500

B $126,100

C $127,000

D $128,500

**(2 marks)**

**The following information relates to questions 47 and 48:**

A company manufactures and sells two products (X and Y) which have contributions per unit of $8 and $20 respectively. The company aims to maximise profit. Two materials (G and H) are used in the manufacture of each product. Each material is in short supply – 1,000 kg of G and 1,800 kg of H are available next period. The company holds no inventories and it can sell all the units produced.

The management accountant has drawn the following graph accurately showing the constraints for materials G and H.

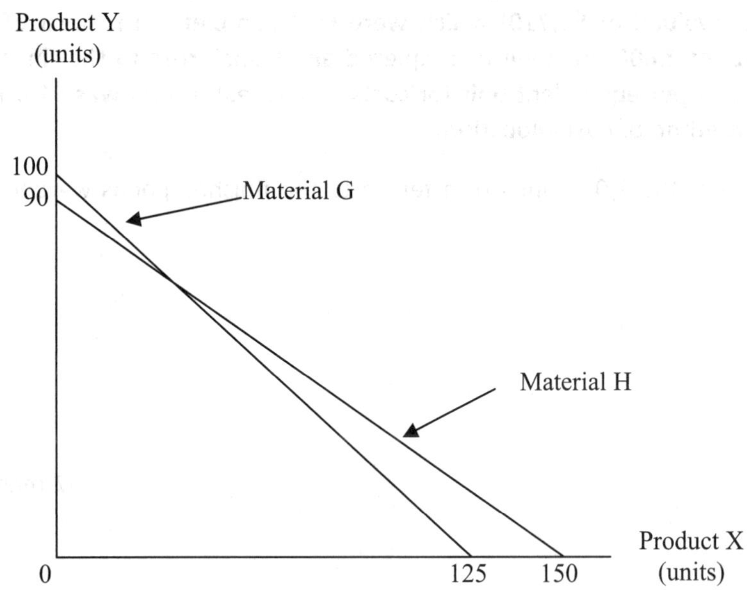


**47 What is the amount (in kg) of material G and material H used in each unit of product Y?**

| | *Material G* | *Material H* |
|---|---|---|
| A | 10 | 20 |
| B | 10 | 10 |
| C | 20 | 20 |
| D | 20 | 10 |

**(2 marks)**

**48 What is the optimal mix of production (in units) for the next period?**

| | *Product X* | *Product Y* |
|---|---|---|
| A | 0 | 90 |
| B | 50 | 60 |
| C | 60 | 50 |
| D | 125 | 0 |

**(2 marks)**

**49 The following statement refers to a quality of good information: The cost of producing information should be greater than the value of the benefits of that information to management.**

Is this statement true or false?

A True

B False

**(1 mark)**

**50 A company which operates a process costing system had work-in-progress at the start of last month of 300 units (valued at $1,710) which were 60% complete in respect of all costs. Last month a total of 2,000 units were completed and transferred to the finished goods warehouse. The cost per equivalent unit for costs arising last month was $10. The company uses the FIFO method of cost allocation.**

What was the total value of the 2,000 units transferred to the finished goods warehouse last month?

A $19,910

B $20,000

C $20,510

D $21,710

**(2 marks)**

Section 4

# ANSWERS TO PILOT PAPER EXAM QUESTIONS

**1 C**

Actual activity – breakeven activity = 1,700 – 1,200 = 500

**2 B**

Financial accounting information is prepared for shareholders, investors and other external stakeholders. Cost accounting is concerned with providing internal management information relating to product costs. Cash budgets record cash received and payments made.

**3 C**

$a = (\Sigma y \div n) - [(b\Sigma x) \div n] = (330 \div 11) - [(0.69171 \times 440) \div 11] = (30 - 27.6684)$

$= 2.3316$ (2.33 to 2 decimal places)

**4 C**

$\{[2 \times 20 \times (4 \times 20{,}000)] \div [0.06 \times 25]\}^{0.5} = 1{,}461$ units

Note the demand figure used in the EOQ formula must be for the same time period as the holding cost per unit. As holding costs are given as annual figures quarterly demand must be multiplied by 4 to represent annual demand.

**5 A**

| | |
|---|---|
| Actual cost | $108,875 |
| Absorbed cost (30,000 × 3.50) | $105,000 |
| Under absorption | $3,875 |

**6 C**

**7 C**

Variable cost per unit: [(170,000 – 5,000) – 135,000] ÷ (22,000 – 16,000) = $5

Total fixed cost (below 17,500 units): [135,000 – (16,000 × 5)] = $55,000

Total cost for 20,000 units: 55,000 + 5,000 + (20,000 × 5) = $160,000

**8 C**

Month 1: Production > Sales  Absorption costing profit > Marginal costing profit

Month 2: Sales > Production  Marginal costing profit > absorption costing profit

A and C satisfy Month 1, C and D satisfy Month 2. Therefore C satisfies both.

**9 C**

Options A and B are incorrect since a flexible budget includes all costs and is not changed to reflect the number of days in the month. A flexible budget may be an update of the fixed budget to reflect actual volume of activity but it does not incorporate actual costs. Thus the answer is option C.

**10 C**

| | *Normal loss litres* | *Actual loss litres* | *Abnormal loss litres* | *Abnormal gain litres* |
|---|---|---|---|---|
| Process F | 5,200 | 6,100 | 900 | – |
| Process G | 1,875 | 1,800 | – | 75 |

**11 A**

Contribution per unit (CPU): (80 × 0.45) = $36

Break even point (units): (99,000 ÷ 36) = 2,750

Margin of safety: (4,000 – 2,750) = 1,250 units

**12 D**

The stores is a service cost centre and stores costs will be indirect.

**13 B**

(150 × 40) + (250 × 53) = $19,250

**14 A**

The correlation coefficient must be between +1 (perfect positive correlation) and -1 (perfect negative correlation)

**15 A**

Statement 1 is correct. A budget manual is needed at the beginning of the process to outline key assumptions, dates, preparation deadlines, etc.

**16 A**

Raw material is a variable cost so the total cost line must begin at 0. Hence option B is incorrect. Option C illustrates a lower cost per unit above a certain volume. Option D shows a lump discount being given at a certain volume then the cost per unit continuing at the same rate.

**17 C**

Sales commission is not a production cost.

**18 A**

The expected value is the sum of each outcome multiplied by its probability. This is a weighted average of all outcomes. Hence option A is correct. It may or may not equal one of the actual outcomes so options B and D are incorrect. It does not give any information about the range of outcomes so it is not possible to identify the decision maker's attitude to risk.

**19 C**

(300,000 × 0.60) – (400,000 × 0.40) = +$20,000 (profit)

**20 A**

Price variance: (0.50 × 10,500) = $5,250 Adverse

Volume variance: (500 × 8) = $4,000 Favourable

**21 B**

Budgeted production: (19,000 + 3,000 – 4,000) = 18,000 units

Raw materials required for budgeted production: (18,000 × 8) = 144,000 kg

Budgeted raw material purchases: (144,000 + 53,000 – 50,000) = 147,000 kg

**22 C**

A database is the most suitable software for the storage of large volumes of data.

**23 D**

A fall in the ordering cost would reduce the numerator in the EOQ fraction hence EOQ will be lower. With a lower EOQ average inventory will be lower hence holding costs will be lower

**24 B**

Printers and solicitors are likely to use job costing.

**25 B**

Production > Sales Absorption costing profit > Marginal costing profit

Marginal costing profit: {36,000 – [2,000 × (63,000 ÷14,000)]} = $27,000

**26 B**

CPU: (20 ×0.4) = $8

Break even point: (18,000 ÷ 20) = 900 units

Profit when 1,200 units produced and sold: (300 × 8) = $2,400

Or $18,000 × 40% = $7,200 = total contribution at BEP = fixed costs

$1,200 × (20 × 0.4) = $9,600 – $7,200 = $2,400

**27 D**

Moving the objective function out, this is the last point reached in the feasible region.

**28 False**

Rent cannot be directly attributed to a cost unit and is an indirect cost.

**29 D**

Cost per equivalent unit: (480,000 ÷10,000) = $48

Closing work-in-progress valuation: (4,000 × Degree of completion × 48) = 144,000

Degree of completion = (144,000 ÷ 4,000 ÷ 48) = 0.75 = 75%

**30 D**

| | *X* | *Y* |
|---|---|---|
| CPU | $8 | $10 |
| Contribution per hour | $4 | $2.50 |
| Ranking | 1st | 2nd |

Therefore produce and sell the maximum 800 units of X using 1,600 hours and with the remaining 400 hours produce and sell 100 units of Y.

**31 A**

Products are often unique for each customer.

**32 B**

| | $ | |
|---|---|---|
| Actual expenditure | 235,000 | |
| Actual hours × standard rate (24,000 × 10) | 240,000 | |
| Expenditure variance | 5,000 | Favourable |

**33 C**

| | $ | |
|---|---|---|
| Actual hours × standard rate | 240,000 | |
| Standard cost of actual production (3,900 × 6 × 10) | 234,000 | |
| Efficiency variance | 6,000 | Adverse |

**34 False**

There is a fixed overhead expenditure variance but no fixed overhead volume variance.

**35 A**

Inferior quality materials are likely to be cheaper and will lead to a favourable material price variance and possibly an adverse labour efficiency variance. Lower grade workers are likely to be less efficient and lead to an adverse labour efficiency variance.

**36 C**

This is the definition of a principal budget factor.

**37 C**

The dotted line represents fixed costs and the graph represents profit/loss at each level of activity. Total contribution is the distance between the fixed cost line and the profit line (option J). Option G is loss. Option K is profit. Option H is fixed cost.

**38 False**

Information is data that has been processed to be meaningful.

**39 C**

Joint costs apportioned to H: [330,000 ÷ (420,000 + 330,000)] × 350,000 = $154,000 Closing inventory valuation (HH): (30,000 ÷ 330,000) × (154,000 + 66,000) = $20,000

**40 B**

Relevant cost: (8,000 – 5,000) = $3,000

**41 B**

| | | |
|---|---|---|
| Budgeted hours | 5,000 | |
| Actual hours worked | 5,500 | |
| Capacity variance | 500 | hours × 15 = $7,500 Favourable |

**42 C**

Materials can have an opportunity cost. For example, a material may be in short supply and, to use it on a contract, supplies would have to be diverted from other contribution generating work. The contribution foregone would be an opportunity cost.

**43 B**

Overtime cost for 250 hours: (250 × 9 × 2) = $4,500

Cost of diverting labour: 250 × (9 + 5) = $3,500

Relevant cost (lowest alternative) = $3,500

**44 D**

200 units × (3 ÷ 60) × 18 = $180

**45 False -** This is a stepped fixed cost

**46 D**

| Total overhead to cost centre P: | $ |
|---|---|
| Direct | 95,000 |
| Proportion of cost centre X [46,000 + (0.10 × 30,000)] × 0.50 | 24,500 |
| Proportion of cost centre Y [30,000 × 0.3] | 9,000 |
| | 128,500 |

**47 A**

100 units of Y with all of material G (1,000 kg) = 10 kg per unit

90 units of Y with all of material H (1,800 kg) = 20 kg per unit

**48 A**

Total contributions:

A [(0 × 8) + (90 × 20)] = $1,800

B [(50 × 8) + (60 × 20)] = $1,600

C [(60 × 8) + (50 × 20)] = $1,480

D [(125 × 8) + (0 × 20)] = $1,000

**49 False**

The benefits of information should exceed the cost.

**50 A**

| | $ |
|---|---|
| Value of 2,000 units transferred: | |
| 1,700 units × 10 | 17,000 |
| 300 units × 0.40 × 10 | 1,200 |
| Opening work-in-progress value | 1,710 |
| | 19,910 |

Section 5

# PRACTICE SIMULATION QUESTIONS

## QUESTION 1

The following details are available for a company:

| | *Budgeted* | *Actual* |
|---|---|---|
| Expenditure | £176,400 | £250,400 |
| Machine hours | 4,000 | 5,000 |
| Labour hours | 3,600 | 5,400 |

**If the company absorbs overheads using labour hours, then, during the period, overheads were:**

**A** Under-absorbed by £29,900

**B** Under-absorbed by £14,200

**C** Over-absorbed by £14,200

**D** Over-absorbed by £64,990 **(2 marks)**

## QUESTION 2

A company uses process costing in calculating output cost. The following details are available for a particular department in December 20X8. All materials are added at the start of the process:

| | |
|---|---|
| Opening Work in Progress | Nil Units |
| Units started | 10,000 units |
| Closing Work-in-Progress | 1,000 units |
| | 100% complete for materials |
| | 75% complete for conversion |
| Normal loss | 200 units |
| Units completed | 8,000 units |

**If all losses occur at the start of the process, how many equivalent units should be included for materials?**

**A** 7,750

**B** 8,750

**C** 8,800

**D** 9,800 **(2 marks)**

## QUESTION 3

**A principal budget factor is a factor common to all functions in budget preparation.**

A True

B False **(1 mark)**

## QUESTION 4

The management of a company is making a decision which could lead to just three possible outcomes – 'high', 'medium' and 'low' levels of demand. Profit and expected value information are as follows:

| *Outcome* | *Profit* | *Profit x Probability* |
|---|---|---|
| High | $29,000.00 | $7,250.00 |
| Medium | $20,000.00 | $8,000.00 |
| Low | $12,000.00 | $4,200.00 |

**What is the most likely level of profit from making the decision?**

A $19,450

B $20,000

C $20,333

D $29,000 **(2 marks)**

## QUESTION 5

A sunk cost is a relevant cost.

**Is this statement true or false?**

A True

B False **(1 mark)**

## QUESTION 6

The following data is available for a company in period 2.

| | |
|---|---|
| Actual overheads | $225,900 |
| Actual machine hours | 7,530 |
| Budgeted overheads | $216,000 |

**Based on the data above and assuming that the budgeted overhead absorption rate was $32 per hour, the number of machine hours (to the nearest hour) that were budgeted to be worked were:**

A 7,059

B 6,750

C 6,900

D 7,000 **(2 marks)**

## QUESTION 7

**Overhead absorption is a means of attributing total costs to a cost unit.**

**A** True

**B** False **(1 mark)**

---

**The following information relates to questions 8 and 9.**

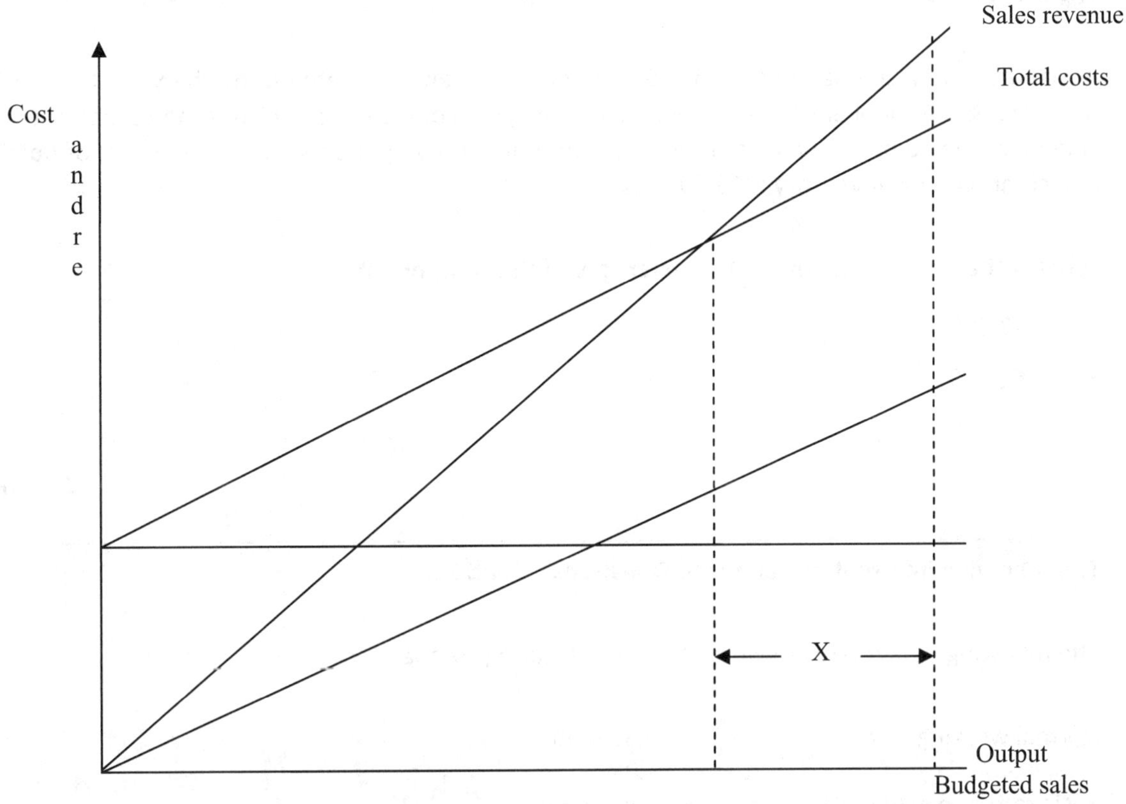


---

## QUESTION 8

**This graph is known as:**

**A** conventional breakeven chart

**B** contribution breakeven chart

**C** semi-variable cost chart

**D** profit volume chart **(2 marks)**

## QUESTION 9

**What does X represent?**

**A** The margin of safety

**B** The profit margin **(1 mark)**

## QUESTION 10

A manufacturing company uses 28,000 components at an even rate during the year. Each order placed with the supplier of the components is for 1,600 components, which is the Economic Order Quantity. The company holds a buffer inventory of 800 components. The annual cost of holding one component in inventory is €3.50.

**What is the Annual Cost of holding inventory of the component?**

**A** €2,800

**B** €4,200

**C** €5,600

**D** €5,700 **(2 marks)**

**The following information relates to Questions 11 and 12.**

The following data relates to work at a manufacturing company:

| | |
|---|---|
| Normal working week | 36 hours |
| Basic rate of pay (direct) | $6.20 per hour |
| Overtime pay | $7.50 per hour |

Last week, the total hours worked by all these workers was 936. The overtime hours worked was 108. All employees worked at least their basic 36 hours.

## QUESTION 11

**The number of workers who worked last week:**

**A** was 23

**B** was 26

**C** was 29

**D** cannot be determined from the above data **(2 marks)**

## QUESTION 12

**The total direct labour charge for the above was:**

A $810.00

B $5,133.60

C $5,803.20

D $6,210.00 **(2 marks)**

## QUESTION 13

A manufacturer of children's toys wishes to increase his C/S (contribution/sales) ratio.

**Which of the following is likely to achieve this aim?**

(i) taking advantage of quantity discounts for bulk purchases of inputs

(ii) introducing training programmes designed to improve labour efficiency

(iii) following the actions of a competitor who has cut prices substantially

(iv) reducing exports to countries where there is intense price competition

(v) offering retailers a lower price if they promote the product more heavily

**A** (ii), (iii) and (v)

**B** (i), (ii) and (iv)

**C** (i), (iii) and (iv)

**D** (ii), (iv) and (v) **(2 marks)**

## QUESTION 14

**Service costing is characterised by high levels of indirect costs as a proportion of total costs and the use of composite cost units.**

**A** True

**B** False **(1 mark)**

## QUESTION 15

A Company has four departments – Assembly, Finishing, Maintenance and Administration. Budgeted data for each department is shown below:

| | *Assembly* | *Finishing* | *Maintenance* |
|---|---|---|---|
| Allocated overheads | $90,000 | $100,000 | $10,000 |
| Direct labour hours | 5,000 | 6,000 | Nil |
| Machine hours | 10,000 | 3,000 | 2,000 |
| Percentage of time spent maintaining machinery | 60 | 40 | Nil |
| Number of staff | 60 | 120 | 10 |

**The most appropriate production overhead absorption rate to use in the Assembly department would be:**

**A** £9.60 per machine hour

**B** £9.90 per machine hour

**C** £17.33 per labour hour

**D** £18.33 per labour hour

**(2 marks)**

## QUESTION 16

Products A and B are manufactured in a joint process. The following data is available for a period:

| | | |
|---|---|---|
| Joint process costs | $30,000 | |
| Output: | Product A | 2,000 kg |
| | Product B | 4,000 kg |
| Selling price: | Product A | $12 per kg |
| | Product B | $18 per kg |

**What is Product B's share of the joint process costs if the sales value method of cost apportionment is used?**

**A** 7,500

**B** 18,000

**C** 20,000

**D** 22,500

**(2 marks)**

**The following data relates to Questions 17 and 18.**

Budgeted production details for November are as follows:

| | Product X | Product Y | Product Z |
|---|---|---|---|
| Units produced | 2,000 | 1,600 | 2,200 |
| Units sold | 1,800 | 1,500 | 2,000 |
| Variable cost/unit | 100 | 80 | 120 |
| Fixed overhead absorbed/unit | 30 | 30 | 50 |
| No. of labour hours | 6 | 4.5 | 5 |

There was no opening stock at the beginning of November.

## QUESTION 17

**Budgeted fixed overheads for November were:**

**A** $810,000

**B** $739,000

**C** $218,000

**D** $199,000 **(2 marks)**

## QUESTION 18

**Which of the following statements is true?**

**A** Absorption costing profit will be $19,000 lower than marginal costing profit

**B** Absorption costing profit will be $71,000 lower than marginal costing profit

**C** Absorption costing profit will be $19,000 higher than marginal costing profit

**D** Absorption costing profit will be $71,000 higher than marginal costing profit **(2 marks)**

## QUESTION 19

The total costs incurred at various output levels in a factory have been measured as follows:

| Output in units | Total cost |
|---|---|
| 25 | £5,500 |
| 30 | £5,450 |
| 33 | £5,550 |
| 44 | £6,000 |
| 48 | £6,500 |
| 52 | £7,000 |

**The variable cost per unit and the Total Fixed Costs are (rounded figures):**

**A** Variable Cost £50 per unit, Fixed costs £4,000

**B** Variable Cost £53 per unit, Fixed costs £4,000

**C** Variable Cost £56 per unit, Fixed costs £4,111

**D** Variable Cost £59 per unit, Fixed costs £4,111 **(2 marks)**

## QUESTION 20

A company makes a product that uses two materials. Standard cost information is given below:

Material A: 2 kg × $7

Material B: 3 litres × $11

In a period 1,300 units were made, and the following actual results were recorded:

Material A: 2,600 kg were bought at a cost of $18,400 and 2,400 kg were used

Material B: 3,900 litres were bought at a cost of $38,800 and 4,000 litres were used.

The company maintains its stocks at standard cost.

**What was the total price variance reported in the period?**

**A** 4,300 (F)

**B** 3,600 (F)

**C** 3,900 (F)

**D** 3,600 (A) **(2 marks)**

## QUESTION 21

Regression analysis is being used to find the line of best fit (y=a + bx) from eleven pairs of data. The calculations have produced the following information:

| | |
|---|---|
| $\sum x$ | 440 |
| $\sum y$ | 330 |
| $\sum x^2$ | 17,986 |
| $\sum y^2$ | 10,366 |
| $\sum xy$ | 13,467 |

And b = 0.69171

**What the value of 'a' in the equation for the line of best fit?**

**A** 0.63

**B** 0.69

**C** 2.33

**D** 5.33 **(1 mark)**

## QUESTION 22

**Which of the following statements IS true when applied to fixed costs:**

**A** overhead costs are always fixed costs

**B** as production levels increase, fixed cost per unit decreases

**C** fixed costs are always irrelevant in a decision making situation

**D** as the level of activity changes, fixed costs will also change **(2 marks)**

## QUESTION 23

**A job is budgeted to require 3,300 productive hours after incurring 25% idle time. If the total labour cost budgeted for the job is $36,300, what is the labour cost per hour (to the nearest penny)?**

**A** $8.25

**B** $8.80

**C** $11.00

**D** $13.75 **(2 marks)**

## QUESTION 24

**Which of the following statement about variable costs is correct?**

Variable costs are conventionally deemed to:

**A** be constant per unit of output

**B** vary per unit of output as production volume changes

**C** vary in total when production volume is constant

**D** vary, in total, from period to period when production is constant **(2 marks)**

## QUESTION 25

The cost card of an electronic component made by DEL Ltd is:

| | $ |
|---|---|
| Direct labour | 2.00 |
| Direct materials | 22.50 |
| Variable overheads | 2.50 |
| Fixed overheads | 3.00 |

The price is set to give a profit margin of 25%.

**The price should be:**

**A** $33.75

**B** $36

**C** $37.50

**D** $40 **(2 marks)**

## QUESTION 26

Four vertical lines have been labelled A, B, C, D at different levels of activity on the following profit-volume chart:

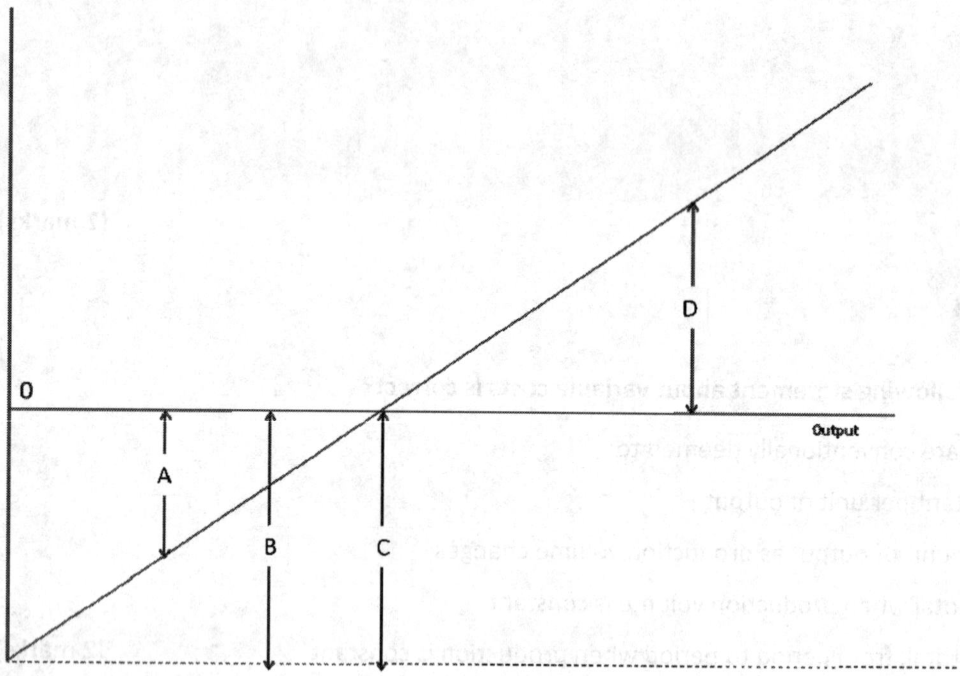


**Which line represents the total contribution at that level of activity?**

**A** Line A

**B** Line B

**C** Line C

**D** Line D

**(2 marks)**

## QUESTION 27

D Ltd operates a total absorption costing system. Budgeted fixed overheads for 2007 were $175,000 and budgeted production was 5,000 units.

**During 2007, the actual fixed overheads amounted to $186,000 and actual production was 6,000 units. Overheads have been:**

**A** under-absorbed by $24,000

**B** under-absorbed by $11,000

**C** over-absorbed by $11,000

**D** over-absorbed by $24,000

**(2 marks)**

## QUESTION 28

A continuous budget is prepared retrospectively.

**Is this statement true or false?**

**A** True

**B** False **(1 mark)**

## QUESTION 29

Below is the standard cost card for one unit of product K.

| | *$/unit* |
|---|---|
| Selling price | 35 |
| Direct materials | 20 |
| Direct labour | 4 |
| Variable overhead | 1 |
| Fixed overhead | 6 |

**Production was 50,000 units and sales 60,000 units. Opening inventory was 25,000 units. The profit calculated using marginal costing was $180,000. The profit using absorption costing is:**

**A** $30,000

**B** $120,000

**C** $210,000

**D** $240,000 **(2 marks)**

## QUESTION 30

**Direct costs are costs that:**

**A** can be directly identified with a product or service

**B** are directly under the control of a manager

**C** are incurred directly the factory is opened

**D** are directly charged to a department **(1 mark)**

## QUESTION 31

A firm has some material which originally cost $49,000. It has a scrap value of $12,500, but, if re-worked at a cost of $7,500, it could be sold for $17,500. There is no other foreseen use for the material.

**The relevant cost of using the material for a special job is:**

A Nil

B $12,500

C $17,500

D $20,000

**(2 marks)**

## QUESTION 32

Caz is considering its options with regard to a piece of machinery which cost $150,000 six years ago. The current replacement cost of that particular machine is $250,000.

Selling the piece of machinery would generate scrap sales of $160,000. Keeping the machine in-house would generate a net income of $175,000.

**The relevant cost of the machine is:**

A $150,000

B $160,000

C $175,000

D $250,000

**(2 marks)**

## QUESTION 33

**A centre which is responsible for managing both costs and revenues is best described as:**

A Revenue centre

B Investment centre

C Profit centre

**(1 mark)**

## QUESTION 34

An industrial bakery manufactures two products, the Brioche and the Croissant, in batches. It uses the same material and labour for both products, and holds no stock. You are given the following information:

| | *Brioche* | *Croissant* |
|---|---|---|
| | € per batch | € per batch |
| Material €4 per litre | 13 | 19 |
| Labour €7 per hour | 35 | 28 |
| Maximum monthly demand | 6,000 | 8,000 |

Each month, 55,000 litres of material and 58,000 labour hours are available.

**Which of the following statements is correct?**

**A** Material is a limiting factor, but labour is not a limiting factor

**B** Material is not a limiting factor, but labour is a limiting factor

**C** Neither material nor labour is a limiting factor

**D** Both material and labour are limiting factors **(2 marks)**

## QUESTION 35

Luke Ltd makes a single product which it sells for $100.00 per unit, on a contribution to sales ratio of 25%. It has fixed costs of $30,000 per month.

**What is its breakeven sales revenue?**

**A** $120,000

**B** $125,000

**C** $130,000

**D** $135,000 **(2 marks)**

## QUESTION 36

**The use of composite cost units is a characteristic of service costing.**

**A** True

**B** False **(1 mark)**

## QUESTION 37

**Which of these statements regarding expected values is correct?**

**A** Expected values can be used to calculate the correlation coefficient

**B** An expected value is a long run average

**C** The project with the largest negative expected value will give you the best return

**D** The project with the lowest expected value should be chosen **(2 marks)**

## QUESTION 38

**Using data from 40 counties in England and Wales, it has been calculated that the correlation between the level of trampoline ownership and the number of neck injuries is 0.75. Which of the statements shown follow this?**

(i) High levels of trampoline ownership in a given county cause high levels of neck injuries.

(ii) There is a strong relationship between the level of trampoline ownership and the number of neck injuries.

(iii) 56% of the variation in the level of neck injuries from one county to the next can be explained by the corresponding variation in the level of trampoline ownership.

(iv) 75% of the variation in the level of neck injuries from one county to the next can be explained by the corresponding variation in the level of trampoline ownership.

**A** (i) and (ii) only

**B** (i) and (iii) only

**C** (ii) and (iii) only

**D** (ii) and (iv) only

**(2 marks)**

## QUESTION 39

K Ltd has published the following profit-volume chart:

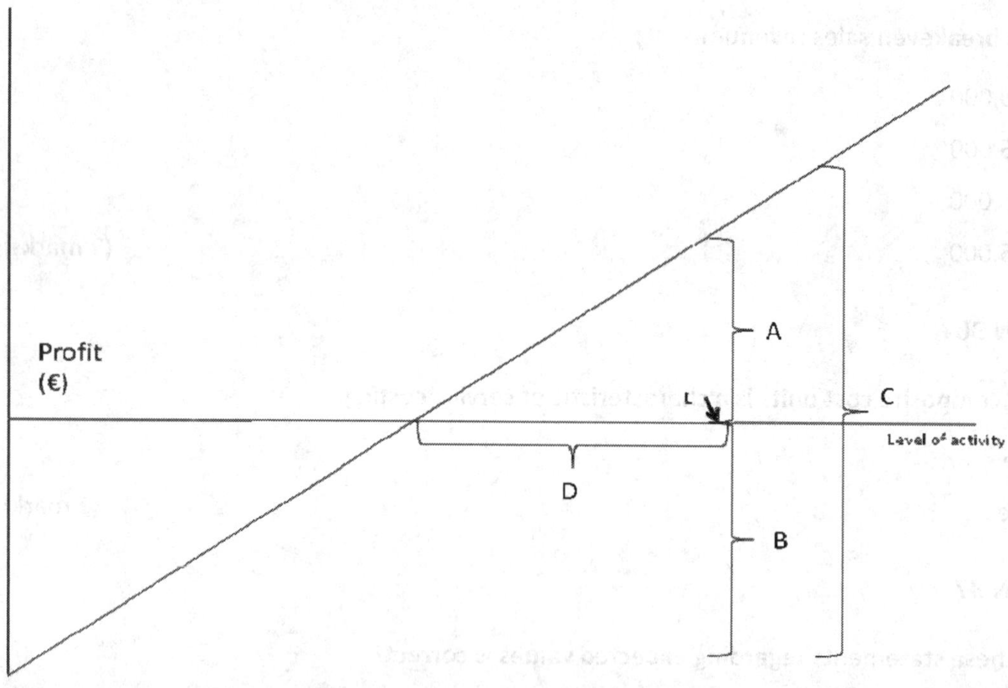


**The contribution at level of activity L can be identified as:**

**A** A

**B** B

**C** C

**D** D

**(2 marks)**

## QUESTION 40

The Widget has a standard labour time of two hours per unit. The standard labour rate is $6 per hour. During one particular month 5,000 units were produced. The actual labour cost was $52,525 for 9,550 hours worked.

**The labour rate variance is:**

**A** $4,775 A

**B** $4,775 F

**C** $7,475 F

**D** $7,475 A **(2 marks)**

## QUESTION 41

A company produces two types of Garden sheds, the Traditional and the Modern, which require 10 and 16 labour hours respectively. The budgeted data for the next period is as follows:

| | *Traditional* | *Modern* |
|---|---|---|
| Sales | 7,500 | 12,000 |
| Opening inventory of finished goods | 1,800 | 2,400 |

Closing inventory of finished goods are expected to be reduced by 50%.

**What are the total budgeted labour hours for the next period?**

**A** 295,200

**B** 267,000

**C** 238,800

**D** 210,600 **(2 marks)**

## QUESTION 42

The following statements refer to spreadsheets:

(1) Spreadsheets can used for budgeting.

(2) Spreadsheets are very useful for word-processing.

(3) Spreadsheets make the manipulation of data easier and quicker.

**Which of these statements are correct?**

**A** (1) and (2)

**B** (1) and (3)

**C** (2) and (3)

**D** (1), (2) and (3) **(2 marks)**

## QUESTION 43

A company uses standard marginal costing. Last month, when all sales were at the standard selling price, the standard contribution from actual sales was $50,000 and the following variances arose:

| | |
|---|---|
| Total variable costs variance | $3,500 adverse |
| Total fixed costs variance | $1,000 favourable |
| Sales volume contribution variance | $2,000 favourable |

**What was the actual contribution for last month?**

**A** $46,500

**B** $47,500

**C** $48,500

**D** $49,500 **(2 marks)**

## QUESTION 44

**A production worker is paid a salary of $650 per month, plus an extra 5 cents for each unit produced during the month. This labour cost is best described as:**

**A** A variable cost

**B** A fixed cost

**C** A step cost

**D** A semi-variable cost **(2 marks)**

## QUESTION 45

A supplier of telephone services charges a fixed line rental per period. The first 10 hours of telephone calls by the customer are free, after that all calls are charged at a constant rate per minute up to a maximum, thereafter all calls in the period are again free.

**Which of the following graphs depicts the total cost to the customer of the telephone services in a period?**

A

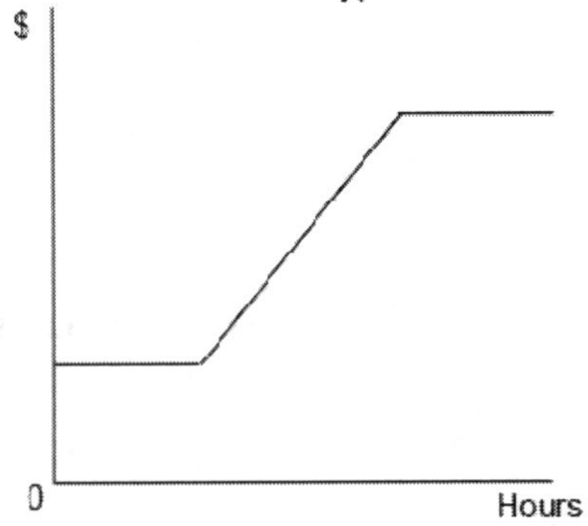


B

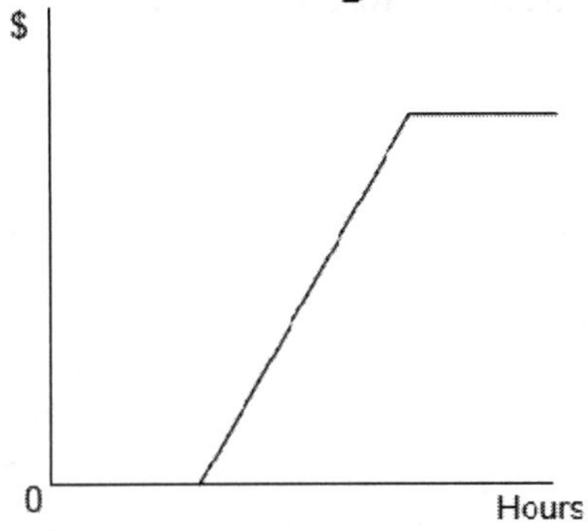


C

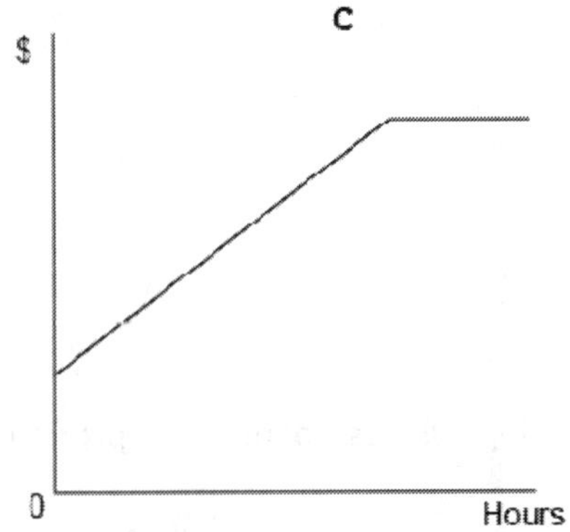


D

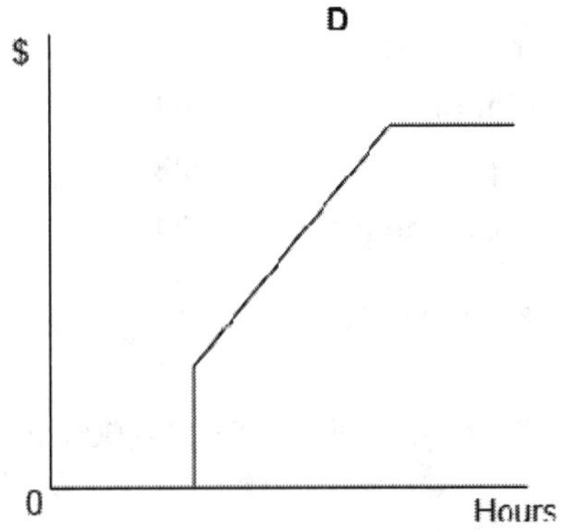


**(2 marks)**

## QUESTION 46

Rogers plc wishes to use a machine for one month on a new contract. The machine cost $120,000 six years ago. When purchased it had an estimated life of ten years and it is being fully depreciated using the straight-line method. It is currently valued at $39,000 and its estimated value at the end of the year is $15,000. The machine is under-used and stands idle for perhaps 30% of its time, but it must be retained for use on similar contracts.

**The relevant cost of using the machine on the new contract is:**

**A** Nil

**B** $250

**C** $812.50

**D** $1,000 **(2 marks)**

## QUESTION 47

A company produces wardrobes which it sells for $300 per unit and has the following breakdown of costs per unit:

| | |
|---|---|
| Direct materials | 120 |
| Direct labour | 62 |
| Direct expenses | 28 |
| Variable overheads | 24 |
| Total variable cost | 234 |

Total fixed costs for the year were $3,000,000 and the building wishes to make a profit of $500,000.

**How many units will the organisation need to produce and sell to achieve this (to the nearest whole unit)?**

**A** 53,000

**B** 53,030

**C** 53,045

**D** 53,060 **(2 marks)**

**The following information relates to questions 48 and 49.**

During the month of December, a manufacturing process incurs material costs of £8,000 and conversion costs of £4,500. 2,000 kgs of material was input. There is a normal loss of 10% and all losses have a scrap value of £1.75 per kg. During the period, 1700 kgs were output to finished goods. Opening and Closing stocks in the process were nil.

## QUESTION 48

**The cost per kg output was:**

A £6.25

B £6.75

C £6.94

D £7.35 **(2 marks)**

## QUESTION 49

**The value of the abnormal loss written off in the profit and loss account will be**

A £675

B £175

C £2025

D £500 **(2 marks)**

## QUESTION 50

Jojo is an assembly worker earning $12 per hour for a basic 35 hour week. Any overtime is paid at a premium of 50%.

In the last four-week period, Jojo was paid for 150 hours. During this time 15 hours were classed as idle due to a machine breaking down. Also included in the number of hours are four hours' overtime spent working for an urgent job at the request of the customer.

**How much should be charged to the production overhead account for the four-week period?**

A $216

B $240

C $288

D $360 **(2 marks)**

Section 6

# ANSWERS TO PRACTICE SIMULATION QUESTIONS

**1 C**

OAR = \$176,400/3,600 = \$49

| | \$ |
|---|---|
| Amount absorbed = \$49 × 5,400 = | 264,600 |
| Actual overhead | (250,400) |
| Over absorbed | 14,200 |

**2 D**

**Process account**

| | Units | | Units |
|---|---|---|---|
| Materials (100% complete) | 10,000 | CWIP | 1,000 |
| | | Normal loss | 200 |
| | | Output | 8,000 |
| | | Abnormal loss | 800 |
| | 10,000 | | 10,000 |

**3 B – FALSE**

A principal budget factor is a factor which limits the activities of the organisation.

**4 B**

The question stated that there were just three possible outcomes for profit in a decision situation. The requirement asked for the most likely level of profits, that is the one of the three possibilities with the highest probability of occurring. The probability of a \$29,000 profit was.0.25 and that of a \$20,000 profit was 0.4.

**5 B**

**6 B**

Budgeted hours = $\frac{\$216,000}{\$32}$ = 6,750 hours

**7 B – FALSE**

It is a method of attributing total production cost centre overheads to a cost unit, not total costs.

**8 A**

**9 A**

**10 C**

{[Buffer inventory + (EOQ ÷ 2)] × Annual holding cost per component}

= [800 units + (1,600 units ÷ 2)] × €3.50 = €5,600

**11 A**

Normal time = 936 – 108 = 828 hours

Number of employees = 23

**12 C**

Direct labour charge is **all** hours (including overtime) at normal rate: 936 × $6.20 = $5,803.20

**13 B**

**14 A**

**15 A**

| | *Assembly* | *Finishing* | *Maintenance* |
|---|---|---|---|
| Allocated o/hs | 90,000 | 100,000 | 10,000 |
| Maintenance | 6,000 | 4,000 | (10,000) |
| | 96,000 | 104,000 | – |

OAR for Assembly department = £96,000/10,000 machine hours = £9.60

**16 D**

| | *Output(kg)* | *Sales value ($)* | *Apportionment of joint costs ($)* | |
|---|---|---|---|---|
| Product A | 2,000 | 24,000 | (24/96) | 7,500 |
| Product B | 4,000 | 72,000 | (72/96) | 22,500 |
| | | 96,000 | | 30,000 |

**17 C**

($30 × 2,000) + ($30 × 1,600) + ($50 × 2,200) = $218,000

**18 C**

All stocks are increasing, so absorption costing profits will be higher by:

($30 × 2,00) + ($30 × 100) + ($50 × 200) = $19,000

**19 C**

| | *Units* | *Total costs* |
|---|---|---|
| High | 52 | £7,000 |
| Low | 25 | £5,500 |
| Difference | 27 | £1,500 |

Therefore, Variable costs = $\frac{\text{£1,500}}{\text{27 units}}$ =£55.56 per unit

By substitution, we find FC = £4,111.

**20 C**

**21 C**

Y = a + bx

330/11 = a + (0.69171 × 440)/11

30 = a +27.66 so a = 2.33

**22 B**

**23 A**

Total hours worked, and paid = 3,300/0.75 = 4,400 hours

Hourly rate = $36,300/4,400 = $8.25

**24 A**

**25 D**

| | |
|---|---|
| Total costs | = $30 |
| Profit margin | = 25%, therefore cost = 75% |
| Price | = $30 ÷ 0.75 = $40 |

**27 D**

| | |
|---|---|
| Overheads incurred | 186,000 |
| Actual absorption $\frac{175,000}{5,000} \times 6,000$ | 210,000 |
| Over-absorbed | 24,000 |

**28 B**

**29 B**

| | |
|---|---|
| Marginal costing profit | 180,000 |
| *Plus* | |
| (15,000 – 25,000) × $6 | (60,000) |
| Equals absorption costing profit | 120,000 |

**30 A**

**31 B**

The original cost of $49,000 is a past cost, or sunk cost, and is therefore irrelevant. The material would not be re-worked, since its value would only increase by $5,000 ($17,500 - $12,500) for a cost of $7,500.

The relvant cost of using the material on the job is, therefore, the opportunity cost of the scrap sale foregone, i.e. £12,500.

**32 C**

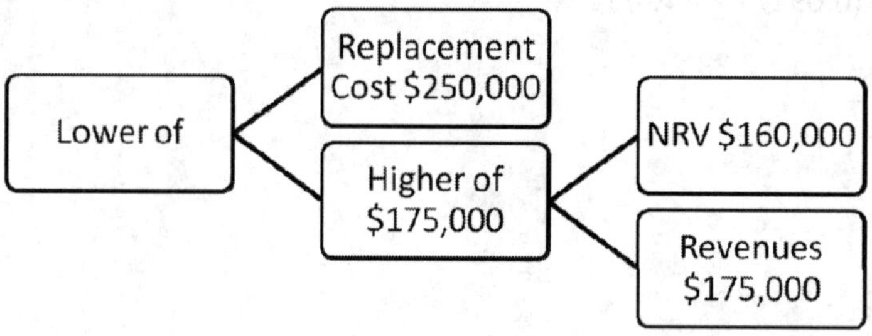


**33 C**

**34 D**

Material required to meet maximum demand:

6000 × (13÷4) + 8,000 × (19÷4) = 57,500 litres

Material available = 55,000 litres. Therefore, material is a limiting factor.

Labour required to meet maximum demand:

6000 × (35÷7) + 8,000 × (28÷7) = 62,000 hours

Labour available = 58,000 hours. Therefore, labour is a limiting factor.

**35 A**

Breakeven sales revenue = Fixed costs ÷ Contribution to sales ratio

= $30,000 ÷ 0.25 = $120,000

**36** **A**

**37** **B**

**38** **C**

**39** **C**

Contribution = Profit + Fixed costs

**40** **B**

| | | |
|---|---|---|
| AH × AR | = 9,550 × $5.5 = 52,525 | |
| **Rate variance** | | **4,775 F** |
| AH × SR | = 9,550 × $6.0 = 57,300 | |

**41** **C**

Budgeted production

| | | |
|---|---|---|
| Traditional | = 7,500 + 900 – 1,800 | = 6,600 |
| Modern | = 12,000 + 1,200 – 2,400 | = 10,800 |
| Labour hours | = (6,600 × 10) + (10,800 × 16) | = 238,800 |

**42** **B**

**43** **A**

| | |
|---|---|
| Sales contribution on actual sales | $50,000 |
| Less: Adverse total variable costs variance | ($3,500) |
| Actual contribution | $46,500 |

No adjustment is required for the favourable sales volume contribution variance, as it will have already been added to the budgeted contribution to arrive at the standard contribution from actual sales ($50,000) given in the question.

**44** **D**

**45** **A**

For the first 10 hours of calls only the fixed line rental is charged therefore the answer cannot be B or D, which show no costs until a number of hours have passed. Graph C shows a variable cost is charged from nil to a maximum number of hours which is incorrect.

**46** **A**

As the machine stands idle but must be retained, there is no future cash flow related to keeping it for the contract. The relevant cost is zero.

**47 B**

Contribution per unit = \$(300 – 234) = \$66

Volume required = $\frac{3{,}000{,}000 + 500{,}000}{66}$ = 53,030

**48 B**

**Process account**

| | Units | \$ | | Units | \$ |
|---|---|---|---|---|---|
| Materials | 2,000 | 8,000 | Normal loss | 200 | 350 |
| Conversion | | 4,500 | Output | 1,700 | 11,475 |
| | | | Abnormal loss | 100 | 675 |
| | 2,000 | 12,500 | | 2,000 | 12,500 |

Average cost = (\$12,500 – \$350)/(2,000 – 200) = \$6.75

**49 D**

**Abnormal loss account**

| | Units | \$ | | Units | \$ |
|---|---|---|---|---|---|
| Abnormal loss | 100 | 675 | Scrap | 100 | 175 |
| | | 675 | P&L | | 500 |
| | 100 | 675 | | 100 | 675 |

**50 A**

Idle time + General overtime = (15 hours × \$12) + ((10 hours – 4 hours) × \$6) = \$216